BISHOP THE
INTERVIEW
GAME

D1380772

THE INTERVIEW GAME

– and how it's played

Celia Roberts

BBC Publications

This book accompanies the BBC Television series *The Interview Game*, first broadcast on BBC 2 from September 1985.

This series was produced by Julian Stenhouse and Jenny Stevens.

Published to accompany a series of programmes prepared in consultation with the BBC Continuing Education Advisory Council.

© Celia Roberts 1985
First published 1985
Reprinted 1985, 1986
Published by BBC Publications,
a division of BBC Enterprises Limited,
35 Marylebone High Street, London W1M 4AA

Typesetting by Wilmaset, Birkenhead, Wirral
Printed in Great Britain by Richard Clay (The Chaucer Press) Ltd,
Bungay, Suffolk
ISBN 0 563 21198 9

Contents

Acknowledgments

This book could not have been written without the help of many colleagues. I should like to thank all those in the Industrial Language Training Service who have contributed so many ideas and insights. In particular I should like to thank Derek Hooper, a co-consultant on the BBC TV series *The Interview Game* and Clarice Brierley, Brian Cheetham, Elisa Christmas, Jenny Ferris, Rod Goddard, Sarah Greenwood, Roger Munns, Pete Sayers, Ann Simpson and Valerie Yates.

I should also like to thank Alix Henley, Tom Jupp and Margaret Simonot for their comments and advice during the writing of this book. I owe an enormous debt to John Gumperz of the University of California, Berkeley for his generosity and enthusiasm over the last ten years.

I should like to thank Raj Jogia and staff of the Oxford City Council who allowed me to try out the ideas in this book before it reached its final form. I should like to thank Janet Marc and Pauline Malone for all their efforts in typing up the book so fast and efficiently. Finally, I should like to thank Julian Stenhouse for his patience, support and care in helping to bring both the TV series and this book into being. Any inaccuracies in facts or distortion of interpretation are entirely my responsibility.

Celia Roberts
Ealing College of Higher Education

June 1985

PART ONE

HOW TO PLAY THE GAME

---

1 Introduction

Aims and approach

This book is about job interviews and it accompanies the BBC TV series *The Interview Game*. It aims to help three groups of people:

○ Anyone who is going for a job interview
○ All interviewers
○ Training officers who run interview training courses

Part One of the book is aimed at all three groups, Part Two is for trainers.

This book has been designed to help both interviewers and candidates. This is because an interview is an encounter in which both sides, interviewers and candidates, have to talk together and need to get on together. Both the interviewer and the candidate will handle the interview better if they know more about what the person opposite is likely to be thinking and how they are probably feeling.

Candidates

This book aims to help candidates understand what goes on beneath the surface of job interviews. Although as candidates you cannot take control in an interview, you can learn about the kinds of questions you will be asked, and what the interviewers are looking for. You can prepare carefully for interviews and you can practice or 'role-play' typical interviews. You may have thought about the questions you will be asked. This book will help you think through, in advance, precisely how you could answer such questions.

Candidates are usually anxious about how they will come across, but have no way of finding out if they are coming across well. If you can persuade a colleague, friend or teacher to role-play an interview with you, covering the main themes of this book, you should feel more prepared, more relaxed and more able to contribute to making the interview more like a conversation and less of an ordeal.

Interviewers

This book aims to help interviewers make the right choice of candidate. The best candidates are not always selected. It is in everyone's interest to make sure that candidates are not rejected for the wrong reasons. This book will help interviewers to communicate to candidates the purpose of the interview questions, to look more analytically at the interview as a procedure for selection and assessment, and to create conditions for a relaxed and fair encounter.

Trainers

Part Two of this book is aimed at trainers. It provides a background to Part One, including references to relevant research, and gives suggestions on how the TV series *The Interview Game* can be used on training courses. Part Two focuses on equal opportunities interviewing and on the interviewing of minority ethnic candidates in particular. The examples and analyses in Part One may also be useful for training purposes, and the Learning Points that follow each example are a helpful summary for course participants.

The organisation of this book

The chapter order does not represent a rigid structure for interviews. They are arranged to reflect the way most interviews go. However orderly the interview appears on the surface, it is not a straight-forward encounter. There is no smooth progression to a neat conclusion. What tends to happen is that different questions cover much of the same ground, and judgements about candidates change from moment to moment with the mood of the interview. Chapters 3–8 illustrate the fact that many aspects of the interview overlap and that the Interview Game is played at many different levels simultaneously.

Chapters 3–8 all include:

Introductions
Examples
Analyses
Learning points

Each example is based on an excerpt from either a real job interview or a simulated interview organised as part of an interviewing training course. Some of the examples are of good practice, some are of poor practice. They should certainly not all be taken as model questions and answers. They are there to illustrate what actually goes on in interviews.

The Learning Points are divided into three types:

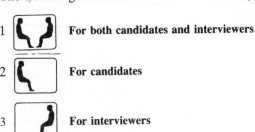

1   **For both candidates and interviewers**

2   **For candidates**

3   **For interviewers**

The figure of the interviewer is symbolic of any number of interviewers sitting together on a panel. It is not intended to suggest that interviews usually are or should be one-to-one encounters. On the contrary, panel interviews have been found to be more reliable than one-to-one interviews. In addition, many Equal Opportunity Employers now require all interviews to be conducted with a panel of interviewers to counteract the effects of individual bias or prejudice.

It is worth explaining what this book is not about. It does not deal with what to wear and how to move the furniture around the interview room. Appearance and arrangements are not unimportant but they are often the only issues discussed in guidance on interviewing. This book concentrates on the talking that goes on in interviews and the judgements that are made on the basis of this talk.

2 The 'Rules' of the Game

A job interview is like a game because, like any game, it has rules. But unlike real games, the 'rules' of the Interview Game are never made clear. They are rules in the sense of being very powerful conventions, or ways of behaving, which govern how interviews run. If interviewers and candidates do not know that these 'rules' are operating, or do not understand their effects then job interviews are likely to be unfair and unreliable.

The unwritten 'rules' of the game

These rules are certainly not listed as ideals to be followed. They may not operate at all in some interviews, and they are not complete. But they are, typically, what most interviewers stick to. They are given here to help interviewers and candidates understand more about the Interview Game. For candidates, knowing the 'rules' may help them to gain at least some control in what will always be an unequal encounter. For interviewers, the chance to stand back and analyse the interview may help them to reassess their own role and the way they conduct the interview.

1 The candidates' suitability for a job is assessed on the basis of how well they can talk in an interview.

2 Qualifications are less important than experience. Often questions about qualifications are routine, and are meant to relax the candidate or are trying to assess the candidates' attitudes or motivation.

3 Interviewers keep power and control but candidates can, at times, take the initiative and talk freely.

4 The interview is an opportunity for candidates to 'sell' themselves but not oversell themselves. Answers should be modestly expressed and backed up with examples.

5 Candidates are expected to be honest about facts, but they can tailor the truth so as not to give a bad impression.

6 Candidates are expected to say that they enjoy their job. New jobs are supposed to be treated as a challenge and not as easy as the current job.

7 Interviewers often do not give any genuine feedback. It is an interview, not a conversation.

8 Candidates should relate their answers to the job on offer, but are rarely invited to do so. Questions from interviewers are usually indirect. The real purpose of the question is hidden.

9 Interviewers may take the smallest negative piece of information from candidates and use it to create a negative impression of the candidate.

10 Interviews go better when the interviewers and candidates establish they have something in common.

The Interview Game

A strange encounter

The job interview is not a natural setting to get to know people and decide on their suitability for a post. It is an encounter full of contradictions:

○ Interviewers have absolute power and control in what is usually a very formal event. Yet there is a pretence of informality and equality.

○ Interviewers have to be fair to everyone. Yet in order to pick one candidate they have to discriminate between candidates.

○ Interviewers are meant to be objective. The outcome of interviews is said to be based on objective standards. But in reality judgements about people are inevitably subjective.

With all these contradictions built into the job interview, indirect questions and 'doctored' answers are what is expected and preferred.

There is a fundamental difference between interview talk and ordinary conversation. In an interview, the interviewers have complete control over how long the talking should go on, what the topics should be and when topics should be switched. Candidates have no rights over the direction and length of the talk. It is hardly surprising, therefore, that most candidates do not see the interview as an opportunity to talk freely and get on in a relaxed way with the people on the other side of the table. But that is precisely what the interviewers expect the candidates to do.

Where there is a panel of interviewers, the chance of talking in a relaxed way and of establishing rapport is even more remote. The different interviewers seem to the candidate to operate as one. But, in fact, each of them is individually sizing up the candidate. The lone candidate is expected to keep the interest of as many as twelve strangers simultaneously, and also to establish rapport with each individual panel member.

Interviewers hold all the power. If they want to establish trust and an atmosphere in which interviewers and candidates can talk together, they must actively help the candidates. They need to relax the candidates, give them some control over how the talking should proceed and give them an opportunity to say what they want to say. The underlying theme of this booklet is that interviews, despite the stress, despite the power of the interviewers, should be a co-operative endeavour. Both sides will gain if there is co-operation and a commitment to communicate clearly.

3 First Impressions

The opening stages of a job interview are a replica, in miniature, of the whole interview. The way the interviewers start the interview affects both the whole tone and structure of the interview, and the way the candidate is judged. So final decisions about the candidates are often determined in these opening stages.

First impressions

First impressions are unavoidable, but both sides can be helped to recognise that first impressions don't have to be lasting impressions. Interviewers should accept that their judgements of candidates may change several times during the interview, and guard against questions that simply reinforce first impressions. Candidates should take every opportunity to use the interviewers' questions to put across those aspects of themselves that are relevant to the job, and show that they are not the one-dimensional figure that walked through the door.

First impressions are crucial. Interviewers have a natural tendency to stereotype candidates on the basis of their appearance, and on information in application forms. These impressions affect the way the interviewers set the scene for the interview and the way they ask questions. They often pick the candidate who looks suitably dressed for the interview rather than the best candidate for the job. In an interview for an engineering apprenticeship, the candidate wearing glasses, suit and tie was asked more favourable questions than candidates dressed less formally, and was judged to be a better candidate.

Opening statements

Opening statements by interviewers about the structure of the interview or about the job are not always as helpful as they could be. Sometimes the interviewer is too nervous to communicate clearly, or makes a vague and rambling statement. The candidate may also be too nervous to listen attentively.

Opening questions

The opening questions and the way candidates respond to them, can either establish a level of co-operation between the interviewers and candidates, or can turn the encounter into an uncomfortable interrogation.

People rarely think about the first impressions the interviewers make on the candidates. But if interviewers are unclear or are perceived as interrogating at the beginning of the interview, this will affect the candidates' performance and their attitude towards the job and the organisation.

Because both sides realise that it's a stressful business, interviewers' opening lines are usually meant to relax the candidate. Since the interviewers hold all the cards in this power game, the candidates need as much opportunity as possible to prepare themselves for operating in this unfamiliar territory. One effective way of making the start of the interview less stressful and more purposeful, is to tell candidates, well in advance of the interview, what the first question will be.

Examples

1 Setting the scene

This interviewer makes a statement at the start of the interview.

Interviewer   Right, before we actually start, can I just explain a bit. I'll ask you some questions about your background and previous experience, okay, and about why you wish to join us. And we'll build up from there through to allowing you to ask questions.

This outline is quite helpful to the candidate but not that helpful. Nervous candidates may not fully take in what is said at the beginning of the interview. Also, the outline given above does not tell the candidate the type of questions that will be asked. The opening questions may still catch the candidates off guard.

A better way of giving candidates a few moments to settle down, is for each member of the interview panel to introduce themselves and say what area they will be asking questions about.

Learning points

Candidates and interviewers

Be clear about the purpose of the interview and prepare yourself for the beginning.

Candidates

Find out, if you can, who will be interviewing you and the physical lay-out of the room.

Use the time the interviewers take for scene-setting, to familiarise yourself with the interviewers.

 Interviewers

If possible show the candidates the interview room. Introduce them to the other interviewers before the interview, or at least tell them who will be interviewing them.

Let the candidates know before the interview what is the first question they will be asked.

Make opening statements as useful as possible. Don't let these statements ramble on.

Start with each member of the interview panel introducing themselves and saying which areas they will be dealing with.

Do not assume that the first impression of candidates is the right one. Wait until candidates have had a real chance to talk before you judge them.

2 Starting with the job

Here is another way of starting the interview.

Interviewer Good afternoon, Miss Morrison. My name's Vaughan and I represent the Borough Maintenance department. First of all I'd like to tell you a little bit about ourselves. In fact we cover the cleansing, transport and technical services which provide a backup service to the other sections: the highways, drainage and building side. In each of the sections there is a support side on the clerical and administration sections. First of all, can we have a look at your application form. Can you tell me something about your last job?

Candidate   I worked in a factory.

Of course, candidates want to know more about the job. But a long description at the beginning of the interview may confuse the candidates. This is even more likely to happen with paraphrases like 'the building side', 'the support side'. A long description may make some candidates feel nervous. They may be worried about remembering everything the interviewer has said in case they are tested on it later. Interviewers should make sure candidates have a description of the job and the organisation before the interview. Long opening statements may stifle candidates and they may give the minimum response. Interviewers should not assume that their first impressions of candidates – for example, that they are not forthcoming – are the right ones.

Learning points

Make sure enough is known about the job, before the interview starts, so there is no wasted time or confusion in the interview.

Before the interview ask for information about the job and, if possible, have a chat informally about the job with someone in the organisation.

Don't worry if you do not pick up everything the interviewer tells you about the job at the start. Ask detailed questions later.

Try to arrange for candidates to have an informal chat before the interview. Make clear whether this is part of the selection process or simply to give information.

Make any comments about the job as factual and precise as possible.

3 Relaxing the candidate

This interviewer tries to relax the candidate by asking about the journey.

Interviewer	Would you like to take a seat?
Candidate	Thank you.
Interviewer	Welcome and thank you for coming. I see you've brought good weather with you. Have you had a good journey?
Candidate	Yes fine, thank you.
Interviewer	Did you drive over?
Candidate	Yes, usual bottlenecks through junctions.
Interviewer	The infamous A6 turnoff?
Candidate	That is correct.

The sole purpose of this series of questions is to relax the candidate. This kind of social conversation can help to relax both interviewer and candidate, provided the candidate recognises that this is its purpose. The aim is to make the interview less of a formal event and more of a conversation. However, it can be just a token gesture before the real business of interrogating the candidate gets under way.

An informal chat before the interview, or an opening question which candidates have been prepared for, are better ways of relaxing candidates.

Learning points

Try to relax those on the other side of the table all the way through the interview.

Remember the interviewers may be nervous too. Making the interviewer feel comfortable may help you get the job.

Don't assume that social chat will necessarily be recognised as such. Don't judge candidates negatively right at the start because they don't respond naturally and easily.

Think about the impression you are making on the candidate. If you are relaxed, they are more likely to be relaxed.

4 Talking about qualifications

A common way of starting off the interview is to take candidates through their application forms.

Interviewer I've had a quick look at your application form. So can we start by talking about your qualifications. You're taking 3 O' levels. How do you think you'll get on?

Candidate Well, I'm taking English, Biology, and Art. I'm quite confident about my Biology and Art, I did quite well in the exams last year. But I'm having to work quite hard at the English.

The issue of qualifications is particularly difficult. Candidates often feel that either too much or too little has been asked about their qualifications. In many interviews this information has already been given in the application form. So questions about qualifications are often routine and are asked to help relax the candidate. However some candidates may consider this is the most crucial part of the interview. Other candidates may feel quite the opposite. Detailed questions about their qualifications may make them feel interviewers are interested in their paper qualifications and are not interested in them as people. Interviewers should guard against starting the interview off in a negative way in order to confirm their negative first impressions. For example:

Interviewer   I see you haven't got many C.S.E.s. Why is it you have so few qualifications?

It is important to start the interview off positively.

Learning points

Be clear about the purpose of questions about qualifications. Are they meant to relax or to probe?

Be prepared to talk about your qualifications in a positive way and show how they are relevant to the job.

Make explicit exactly what it is you want to find out. If you see this stage of the interview as a way of relaxing the candidates, make this clear to them.

If candidates do not have all the expected qualifications, do not spend a lot of time checking up on why not. Move on to asking about their experience. Remember you invited them to the interview despite their lack of conventional qualifications.

4 Experience Talks

Interviewers always ask questions about candidates' work experience. If they think candidates have the 'right' experience, they ask fewer searching questions assuming that candidates can do the job. But sometimes all the candidates seem, on paper, to have appropriate experience. The way they talk about their experience will decide who gets the job.

Talk about work experience

Talking about work experience sounds straightforward but like most things in the Interview Game it is not as simple as it seems. When interviewers ask questions like:

>   What does your job involve?
> or   What do you actually do?

they have certain expectations about the answers. They see all their questions as being obviously related to the job on offer, and expect the candidates to make the connection. Interviewers assume that candidates will talk freely about their work experience, displaying their capabilities and motivation. Interviewers are also looking for more than a straight factual description. They expect to find out something of the candidates' attitudes and opinions as they talk about their work experience. If candidates are not familiar with these expectations then their answers may well be judged as uninformative and the candidates may be assessed as lacking motivation or enthusiasm.

Awkward questions

Often interviewers will ask questions which require candidates to explain or justify themselves:

> Why did you leave that job?
> *or* Did you have any difficulty with. . . ?
> *or* Would you have preferred to. . . ?

It is quite reasonable for candidates to admit to certain difficulties and not do a total cover-up. However, the shrewd candidates try to make the interviewer feel comfortable. Interviewers feel more comfortable if they have found out something positive about the candidates. Sudden or strange job changes, years without promotion or other difficult moments from the past need to be accounted for in a way that sounds positive. Interviewers expect candidates to be honest about facts, but one of the accepted conventions of the Interview Game is to give plausible reasons and explanations for what happened in the past. This is to avoid giving a bad impression.

What if . . .

When candidates don't appear to have the right experience, they are often asked a lot of questions aimed at finding out how they would cope with a particular situation in the job on offer. For example:

> What would you do if. . . ?
> How would you feel about a situation where. . . ?

These hypothetical questions are extremely difficult to answer. Candidates may be quite at a loss what to say. They are required to imagine themselves in a situation they do not know and are expected to be quite precise but not too dogmatic about what they would do. However, candidates who answer hypothetical questions by quoting from their past experience usually have their answer rated as a sensible answer.

Examples

1 Learning from the past

This interviewer wants to find out how the candidate makes decisions and sorts out her priorities.

Interviewer Presumably, during your spell as a production manager, sometimes you were faced with conflicting demands from different quarters. Could you describe some kind of a situation like that which you faced?

Candidate Well, there were times when the sales team didn't consult the production staff and they went out and brought in a lot of business, which we couldn't cope with. So there was pressure to try and please our customers, and produce more than we were able to.

Interviewer Can you tell me something about your approach to coping with that sort of situation, how you dealt with that?

Candidate It depended on the operations director. If he said it had to be done, then it had to be done. We would plan the day, plan what needed to be done urgently and when it could be done.

This interviewer's questions lead to revealing answers, and help the candidate to talk directly about her experience. By talking about what she did the candidate reveals what the interviewer is looking for: the ability to plan and make priorities. Also, the interviewer does not burden the candidate with a string of questions all at the same time. The questions are carefully staged. First he asks the candidate to describe a situation. Then, secondly and separately, he asks her to explain how she dealt with it. The candidate answers with a clear example of conflicting demands. In her second answer she shows that she has responsibilities for planning, but is aware of the limits of her authority.

Learning points

Candidates and interviewers

Talk about actual experiences and relate the questions and answers explicitly to the job on offer.

Candidates

Pick examples from your work experience which can be readily understood by interviewers and show their relevance to the job on offer.

Remember interviewers are looking for personal qualities and not just facts.

Interviewers

Ask candidates about their actual experiences. Ask them to give specific examples.

Ask one question at a time. Make the questions progressively more specific.

2 A mix of fact and opinion

This interviewer's question requires the candidate to sum up four years working in the finance section of an international company.

> *Interviewer* Can you tell me about your four years with Williamsons?
>
> *Candidate* I worked in the head office, in the city, and, as you can imagine, that was a very large office. The different sections are

very much split up, so at first I didn't have very much idea about what was going on, but I quite enjoyed it. At the beginning I worked in accounts. Then I moved on to computer terminal work and data processing. At one stage I worked in the senior manager's office, which was a separate section within the main office. In fact, over the period, I worked in all the main departments which I found very enlightening. I think my experiences there really made me grow up and, I have to admit, I really enjoyed my time there.

This interviewer is looking for facts about the candidate's work experience. The candidate seems to know how much to say and at what level of detail to describe her job. She quickly sets the scene and then she shows that she has a wide range of experience.

The interviewer is also looking for evidence from which to assess her personality and motivation. Although this is not made explicit in the question, the candidate knows instinctively that she needs to weave opinions and feelings into her factual description. She evaluates the job and its benefits for her, along with the facts about what she actually did.

Without either side being aware of it, an interview often goes well when there is a balance maintained between fact and feeling. The straightforward factual question is best answered by building in some attitude or opinion. In the same way answers to questions about feelings need some facts or some analysis to back them up. This blend of fact and feeling is a helpful device for candidates to use when they need to avoid giving a bad impression. They cannot change the facts (like a gap in their work record) but they can explain them in a positive way.

Learning points

Answers should be a blend of facts and feelings.

Be ready to give views about your experience. Remember facts alone won't tell interviewers enough about you as a person and your suitability for the job.

Talk directly about your own personal experiences and mention briefly how your job fitted in with the whole enterprise.

Recognise that 'enjoying' work is a convention of the Interview Game.

Try to talk about a positive aspect of those areas which interviewers may judge as your weak points.

If candidates only give facts in an impersonal way, explain that questions about experience are also to find out about personal attributes such as capability and motivation.

3 What would you do if. . . .

This interview is for the job of bus conductor. The interviewer asks a hypothetical question to find out how the candidate would handle awkward passengers.

Interviewer   Have you given any thought to how you'd deal with the public? If you've got trouble with people who've not paid up the full

	fare? Have you thought about that and how you deal with those type of things?
Candidate	I think I have, but it depends on the situation. I mean I can't comment on it unless it has happened.
Interviewer	No, but would you feel that you should stop the bus right away and deal with them, or just carry on or. . . .
Candidate	It would depend. But working in a shop we get that all the time – they demand a reduction on the price when there's nothing wrong with the garment. And when this happens we follow procedure within the company and explain when it is possible to give a reduction.
Interviewer	Good. So you've got some experience of coping with awkward situations. Good.

This candidate's first answer shows that she is at a loss what to say. But in her second answer she abandons trying to imagine what she might do and instead refers to her past experience. As a result, she shows she can handle awkward situations.

Where someone's experience is obviously appropriate, interviewers tend to ask fewer hypothetical questions. When there are doubts about candidates' suitability, because their experience does not seem to fit, more hypothetical questions are asked. The more doubts there are about the candidate, the longer and more involved the hypothetical questions become. It is quite common for long and complicated questions to be met by short answers because candidates simply cannot anticipate how they would react.

Many interviewers find it hard to resist asking hypothetical questions. But this type of question should be avoided for two reasons. Firstly candidates often respond in a vague way because they do not know enough about the job to be more specific. Secondly hypothetical questions only test the candidates' ability to talk about imaginary situations. They do not test their potential for handling difficult situations.

Learning points

Hypothetical questions don't help either side. Talk instead about past experiences and relate them to the job on offer.

Don't be trapped by hypothetical questions. Use the past to talk about the future.

Don't ask hypothetical questions. Usually the answers are not helpful. Ask candidates to talk about their past experiences and encourage them to relate them to the job they have applied for.

4 Being analytical

In many job interviews candidates are judged not only on the content of what they say but on whether they can give an analytical and balanced answer. They may be asked questions that are topical or political or questions that require the candidate to be analytical about their work experience. Here the candidate is being questioned about a job in a personnel department.

Interviewer   What does 'keeping something confidential' mean to you?

Candidate   Well, it means basically that whatever information you have about an employee is dealt with between the employee and the relevant management, not with any of the other employees. It's information that should be kept confidential.

Interviewer   Why do you think that's important?

Candidate   Well, lots of people have problems, and it's important because if you do have good staff and they do have problems then they know that it's just between them and the employer. As opposed to anyone else. And I suppose it would make them more confident in you as a manager.

The candidate is being assessed here on his ability to talk in an analytical way, rather than how trustworthy he is. Candidates who are able to talk well about abstract concepts will be able to answer this type of question well.

Learning points

Recognise that the purpose of many questions is to assess candidates' ability to give analytical and balanced answers.

Be ready to give reasons, define terms, compare different experiences in a way that shows you have thought about them.

Check the purpose of each question and the demands it puts on the candidate. Are the skills needed to answer the question really necessary for the job?

5 The Hidden Message

Hidden messages in conversation

We are all a good deal less direct in the way that we talk to each other than we may realise. There is often a hidden message in what we say. One reason for this is that in most of our conversations we are doing a balancing act between two different ways of behaving. On the one hand we want to get on with other people, gain their agreement and approval and not offend them. On the other hand, we want to protect ourselves and not necessarily give away what we really think and feel. Coping with these contradictions makes our conversation indirect. Think how often people ask questions like 'Can you do it?' when in fact the hidden message is an order: 'Do it'.

Hidden messages in interviews

Interviews are even more contradictory and compli- cated than the average conversation. Interviewers are expected to be fair to everyone, but they have to discriminate between candidates. Their individual feel- ings and attitudes are not supposed to interfere with the process of selection. Interviews are meant to be objective and the ritual of set questions and answers often gives them an appearance of objectivity. In reality, however, judgements about people are inevitably subjective. Managing these contradictions makes interviewers more indirect, and can make the whole interview a mystifying experience for the candidates.

Interviewers usually do not realise how much of their questioning has a hidden message. Even if they are aware, they feel they must not 'give the game away' by letting the candidate in on the real purpose of their questions. Whether interviewers are deliberately indirect or not, the result of so many hidden questions is to favour the candidates who know the 'rules' of the Game already. By keeping things hidden, interviewers are, right from the start, discriminating in favour of the conventional candidate with the expected background and the preferred answers.

Before an interview, candidates regularly say they do not know what to expect. They simply present themselves and hope for the best. But the interviewers have a clear picture of what they are looking for. Unfortunately this is not normally revealed to the candidate. For example, a typical checklist of qualities in the interviewers' heads, or on paper, would include:

Personality
Reliability
Attitude to authority
Ability to work independently
Judgement
Sense of responsibility
Ability to work with or manage others
Ability to communicate

But the candidates have no such checklist. They sit empty handed on one side of the table, while the interviewers sit on the other side and shuffle papers covered with information.

So the whole interviewers' 'agenda' is hidden from the candidate. The interviewers' line of questioning has a hidden purpose that the candidate may not pick up on. Individual questions also have a hidden meaning. Set questions like 'Why do you want this job?', which are apparently direct and straightforward, are often the hardest to answer. The hidden message in the question is 'What skills and experiences would you bring to this job?' A question like 'What does your job involve?' is only easy to answer if candidates know what the interviewers are looking for. They are looking for qualities like reliability and enthusiasm, but this hidden message is often hard for candidates to recognise. Candidates who fail to pick up the hidden message are often judged by interviewers as lacking intelligence or not being good communicators.

Embarrassment

An interview is not a natural or comfortable way for people to find out about each other. Interviewers often feel awkward and embarrassed. Embarrassment often makes people more indirect and as a result the candidate may be misled:

Interviewer We'll have a little chat so I can get to know you a little better.

But an interview is a lot more than 'a little chat'.

Embarrassment can also lead to interviewers relying on jargon, or vague bureaucratic language, especially at the beginning of the interview. The interviewer may, unthinkingly, use phrases that candidates may find bizarre or inappropriate like:

Park yourself here
Fire away
Vis-a-vis
Be that as it may

Interviewers should avoid using any kind of jargon or vague expressions. These prevent clear communication.

Examples

1 Hidden line of questioning

This interview is for a job involving shift work. The interviewer switches from one hidden line of questioning to another.

Interviewer	Now you'll be working out of doors a lot, are you quite healthy? You don't have any medical problems?
Candidate	No.
Interviewer	You've already mentioned you're married – any family?

Candidates are rarely told when the interviewer is changing topics. Here the interviewer finishes the topic of health, and moves on to the topic of working unsocial hours. But the candidate cannot tell whether the questions about his family link back to the topic of health or are introducing a new topic.

Interviewer	You've already mentioned you're married – any family?
Candidate	Three children.
Interviewer	And where are you living, your own place or . . .

Candidate	My own place.
Interviewer	Now you know the unsocial hours. Your wife, how is she going to feel about the four o'clock starts?

Often candidates don't know whether or not they should be looking for connections between the questions. In this example, the interviewer asks the candidate about his family and where he lives. The interviewer's aim is to find out how he will react to unsocial hours. But the candidate has no idea what the questions are leading up to.

This obscure line of questioning can unnerve candidates or even offend them. If candidates cannot see the purpose behind a string of questions they may be unable to give good answers.

Learning points

Candidates and interviewers

Watch out for the hidden purpose behind a series of questions and clarify their purpose.

Candidates

Try to work out what the interviewers are looking for in their line of questioning.

Interviewers

Remember your line of questioning may seem irrelevant, bizarre or even offensive to the candidate. Make the purpose of the questions explicit.

2 Private and confidential

This interviewer wants to find out what arrangements the candidate would make for her child if she got the job on offer.

> *Interviewer*   You're married and you have a young daughter. Looking at this job, how is this going to affect your home life?
>
> *Candidate A*   Well, it will affect us, obviously but to my mind, it's necessary. I need the stimulation to go out to work and it will help financially. I know a child minder who's looked after her before and they get on very well.

Another candidate answered the same question very differently.

> *Candidate B*   I'm quite prepared to discuss my domestic arrangements, but I would like to know first whether all candidates, both male and female, are being asked the same question.

A lot of questions at interviews deal with private and personal matters. These can be embarrassing and interviewers often deal with embarrassment by becoming more indirect. Many questions about child care arrangements are unnecessary and unlawful. Interviewers are often aware or half-aware of this, and ask obscure questions to check on child care and plans for having babies. Here the candidate recognises that the question is not really about how she would manage at home, but how she would manage at work. She answers the implied question by explaining that she has a suitable childminder. The convention is for interviewers to seem concerned about how people cope with their domestic pressures. In fact, they want to know whether home circumstances will interfere with attendance and performance at work.

The Equal Opportunities Commission considers that any questions about child care and having babies, asked only of women, are unlawful. Such questions could be used as evidence against employers, in industrial tribunals.

Learning points

Questions about personal circumstances should only be put, and answered, if they are absolutely necessary and are fair to all candidates.

Recognise the hidden purpose behind indirect questions about your home, family and lifestyle. You could refuse, politely, to answer such questions if interviewers cannot explain their relevance and their fairness to all the candidates.

Check the necessity and legality of asking about personal and essentially private matters. How would you like to answer such questions in an interview?

3 Hidden meanings

There is one crucial question that is almost always asked in job interviews. It's a question that can be expressed in many different ways:

Why are you interested in this particular job?
What are you looking for in a job like this?

Why do you want to leave your present job?
Why a change now?
What brings you to us at this stage in your career?

All these questions are expecting an answer that will 'sell' the candidate to the interviewers. The question can be rephrased as:

What particular skills, experience and interest do you have which make you think you are particularly suited to this job and could do it well?

In the two examples here the questions are even more indirect because they are phrased in a way which encourages candidates to talk about what they will get out of the job, not what they can give to it.

Interviewer A   What is it about the job that attracted you?

Candidate A   I think the job carries on where I left off – nearly two years ago. I think I can cope with it and for me it would be a means to an end – a career.

Interviewer B   What do you think working for us will offer you?

Candidate B   Longer holidays I think – and an easier life – not so much aggravation.

Interviewers expect candidates to display their motivation. Candidate A knows this 'rule' of the Interview Game. He shows that he is motivated by claiming that he has a long-term career in mind. Candidate B does not pick-up on the hidden message and answers the question at face value. He also does not know another 'rule' of the Interview Game:

Don't admit that the job on offer is easier than your current job. New jobs are supposed to be a challenge.

Learning points

Make sure that answers to all 'Why do you want this job?' questions, give evidence of experience, skill and motivation.

Answer these set questions by showing what makes you a suitable candidate for the job. Explain why the job interests you, and why you think you are capable of doing it.

Make the purpose of questions explicit. If your questions are indirect you will discriminate against candidates who don't know the 'rules' of the Game. Explain that you want to know what particular experience and skills the candidate could bring to the job.

4 Hidden signals

Interviewers want to establish a smooth and comfortable flow of questions and answers. Maintaining a smooth flow is done in several ways. One way is for the interviewer to make leading statements rather than questions so that the interview sounds less like an interrogation.

Interviewer   I see from your form you enjoy community work and sport.

Candidate   Yes, I've kept up my swimming since my schooldays. I now run a local club for handicapped swimmers in the neighbour-hood.

In this example the interviewer makes a leading comment that includes a hidden signal for the candidate to talk about her experiences and not wait for a direct question.

Interviewers also use signals such as pausing, tone of voice, intonation and body language to direct the course of the interview. These are all hidden messages in the sense that the message lies not in *what* we say but *how* we say it. In this example the interviewer repeats the word 'Accounts' in a rising tone of voice:

Candidate . . . and I worked in the Accounts Department as well.
Interviewer . . . Accounts?

This rising tone of voice is an invitation to the candidate to elaborate on his experience. However, some candidates may not pick up on this signal and may interpret the repetition as a confirmation that they have been understood. Alternatively interviewers may simply look at the candidate enquiringly and assume that the candidate recognises the look as an invitation for them to elaborate.

In this last example the interviewer says 'Fine' with a falling tone of voice and then sums up what the candidate has just said.

Candidate . . . and I think it would be interesting and would further my ability to manage people.
Interviewer Fine. So, you feel you've got management skills.

The falling tone of voice and the summing up are both signals that the candidate has said enough, thank you, on that topic and the interviewer wishes to move on.

These are hidden signals which some candidates may mistakenly take as encouragement to continue.

Learning points

Look out for how things are said as well as what is said.

Check with the interviewer if you are not sure whether you have said enough.

If candidates don't respond to your signals for encouraging or discouraging more talk, indicate clearly when they should elaborate or when they have said enough.

6 Getting On Together

As part of the business of everyday life, we 'size each other up' all the time. We do this on the basis of appearance, information discovered during the conversation and the impressions which people make on us as we converse. This 'sizing up' is done quite unconsciously. Similarly in an interview, where the interviewers' task is to make judgements, the factors that lead to a decision are often unclear. When interviewers get on with the candidates they tend to judge them as suitable for the job, because they feel they will 'fit in' with the organisation.

Having something in common

The candidates' chances are helped when both sides find they have something in common. This recognition helps both sides feel more relaxed. They may find they grew up in the same area, are both members of the same club, or have some other aspect of experience or background in common. Interviewers tend to favour candidates when the interview is friendly and comfortable, and when interviewers feel they have really engaged with the candidates. Candidates will be judged as 'fitting in well with us' if what they say seems relevant and clear, if they say the right amount, and if they can pick up on the hidden message behind the questions.

Establishing rapport

In a conversation, the listener would be expected to listen carefully and reply to the speaker. In interviews, interviewers don't feel they have to react in the same way. This lack of response makes candidates feel uncertain, and they are less likely to present themselves in the best possible light. It should be the interviewers' responsibility to help establish rapport by actively listening to the candidate and giving feedback. Interviewers can make the interview more like a conversation and less like an interrogation. Although, in theory, interviews are about objective assessments, in practice they are about rapidly making some kind of relationship with the person opposite.

It is only when the interview is running smoothly that the interviewers feel comfortable. And it is only when the interviewers feel comfortable that the candidates will be judged in a positive way. In theory interviewers are expected to make the candidate feel comfortable. In reality, it's the candidate who needs to make interviewers feel comfortable.

Examples

1 Feedback

Active listening
This interviewer shows that she is interested in what the candidate has to say by commenting on the candidate's answer.

Interviewer You've worked as a care assistant and in summer camps. Each time you have taken on more responsibility than the job actually demanded. How did that happen?

Candidate It's been the sort of situation where you can make of it what you will. And if I'm given that sort of opportunity, I tend to take it. So I've tried to do as much as possible.

> *Interviewer*   So it's really been on your own initiative that you've taken on responsibilities and not because you were specifically asked to do so?

In this kind of feedback, the interviewers comment positively with expressions like 'So you enjoyed it', 'That must have been very demanding'. Comments like these show the candidate that the interviewer is listening properly. This kind of feedback is much more helpful than potentially misleading comments like 'OK', or 'Fine' which often simply signal that the particular question and answer sequence is finished. If either side feels the candidate's answer was not complete or adequate then they should say so directly. This gives candidates another chance to answer the question.

Summing up

A candidate has just described how he set up a club.

> *Interviewer*   You obviously enjoyed doing that. And I'd be right in saying if you hadn't organised it and done it yourself, it wouldn't have happened at all?

In this type of feedback, interviewers sum up what they think is the candidate's main message. This helps both sides ensure that they are on the right track. There is no point in candidates and interviewers talking past each other and not stopping to check that what the candidates intended to say was interpreted correctly by the interviewers.

Learning points

 Candidates and interviewers

Take every opportunity to make the interview more like a conversation.

Candidates

If you are not sure what interviewers are asking, you seek clarification. Take opportunities to pick up on comments and suggestions that interviewers make. Don't let the interview become an interrogation.

 Interviewers

Listen and respond to what the candidates say as if it was a conversation. Don't sit in silent judgement over them. Confirm with the candidate that you have understood what they meant.

2 Something in common

Both sides feel comfortable in this interview because the candidate has a relative who works in the firm.

Interviewer   Have you got any friends or relatives in the company who have told you about the facilities we offer?

Candidate   Yes. My father works in North East Area Office, so I know more or less about them.

Interviewer   Good. That cuts down on the questions I need to ask. You'd obviously get along well on the social side. That's good. It helps people to settle in and do their job better.

This interviewer's task is made easier because he can assume a lot about the candidate's knowledge of the job and the social life. The candidate is almost part of 'the club' already.

Having something in common is rather like the 'old school tie' network which was typically part of the job interview in British colonial life:

'Theophilus himself has no doubts as to why his first job interview with a Dunlops Director went off so well; "He asked me one or two questions as to where I'd been born and what my parents were and so on and then he said, 'What's that tie you've got on?' I said, 'It's the Harlequin Rugby Club, Sir.' And he said 'You'll get some rugger out there' – and that was my interview." '[1]

Clearly this is an unfair and absurd way of selecting candidates.

Learning points

Having something in common helps interviews to go more smoothly.

If you do find you have something in common with the interviewers don't rely on it to get you the job.

Guard against making negative judgements because of the differences between you and the candidate. If you feel there are great differences, make a point of looking for experiences, background or interests that you may share with the candidates.

The best candidate for the job may not be the person you have most in common with.

[1]In *Tales from the South China Seas* edited by Charles Allen (1983, André Deutsch).

3 Making contact

There are many jobs where candidates will need to show an ability to get along well with people. This interviewer describes to a researcher how he finds out whether candidates will be good with people:

'It's very difficult to try and test for skills in dealing with the public. You can only do it by judging their type of personality: you judge that people can handle the public if they can relate to you. If they can be friendly with you, they can be friendly with the public.'

Interviewers are often looking for a friendly and outgoing manner from candidates, particularly if the job requires dealing with the public. Candidates' ability to get on well with difficult members of the public, or handle people they will have to supervise, is judged by their ability to relate to interviewers. This happens in all interviews. Candidates are judged on how they talk in one setting – a formal interview – for how they would perform in another setting – the work place.

It's true that candidates who get on well with interviewers stand a much better chance of getting the job. But interviewers should not assume that candidates can handle the public well because they get on well with the interviewers. A more reliable way of assessing candidates is to find out about their past experience of handling people, or to set up a simulation exercise.

Learning points

Interviews are likely to go better if both sides can find a way of getting on with each other.

Don't take a passive role or assume the interview is only about giving facts about yourself. Make sure you know how much of the job involves working with other people.

Don't assume that the candidates know that their ability to relate well to people in the job is being judged by how well they relate to the interviewers.

Ask candidates about their experience of working with people. Don't judge how friendly they might be in the job by their manner in the stressful atmosphere of a formal interview.

4 Did it go well?

Interviewers and candidates may have very different perceptions about whether an interview went smoothly or not. Here, in separate discussions after an interview, a candidate and an interviewer express different reactions to the same encounter.

Candidate   I think the interview went very well, very smoothly. I was able to talk freely. I think once or twice they asked me quite controversial, political questions. They wanted to find out if I was in favour of trade unions or not. But apart from that it was a very good interview. I think I'll get the job.

Interviewer   I don't think he's suitable for the job. He didn't seem a very motivated person. He was not very dynamic, not very forthcoming.

Interviewers are often told to encourage candidates to talk freely. However, simply talking a lot does not guarantee a good interview. Candidates who think they are talking freely may in fact be judged as 'rabbiting on', or not sticking to the point. It is more important for candidates to make their contributions relevant. Sometimes as candidates' answers get longer they get more vague. This can happen when they are asked political or topical questions, like for example, their attitude to an industrial dispute. Candidates often give a vague answer so as not to get involved in anything too controversial. Interviewers may be far more interested in whether candidates can give a balanced answer – putting both points of view. This kind of balanced answer is more likely to make interviewers feel comfortable.

Learning points

Interviews should be an opportunity to talk freely, but both sides need to be clear about how much to say and the purpose of all this talk.

Try to connect with the interviewers and capture their interest. Don't just talk a lot for its own sake.

Make it clear why you are asking questions about politics or current issues.

Don't blame the candidates for talking too much if that is what you encouraged them to do.

7 The Power of Questions

Good questioning helps the candidate to perform well. By the same token, poor, confused or unfair questioning will prevent the candidate from performing well. Often, interviewers blame the candidates for what is in fact their own poor performance. Whether an interview goes well or badly depends on what both sides do.

The questions that are asked, and how they are asked, will have an enormous influence on whether an interview goes well or badly. Questions are so powerful because interviewers have the right (with some limitations imposed by law) to ask whatever they want, however they want. Unless candidates can find a way of taking the initiative themselves, the interviewers control the questioning, and so control the whole tone and direction of the interview.

The interviewers' questions also form and shape the way the candidate appears to the interviewers. Anyone who has been through an interview has probably felt that they did not come across as their real self. Interviewers who later meet candidates in a setting very different from that of the formal interview may hardly recognise them as the same people.

Good interviewing technique allows the candidate to talk at least 60% of the time. This often does not happen. If interviewers are very impressed with a candidate, they tend to talk more – trying to 'sell' the job to the candidates. But interviewers also talk more when they are unhappy about the candidate, and spend a lot of time warning the candidate off the job.

Open questions

The most effective way of encouraging candidates to talk is to ask open questions. These are questions which cannot be answered with just 'Yes' or 'No'. For example:

> How did you . . . ?
> Why did you decide to . . . ?
> Can you tell us about . . . ?

Open questions allow candidates to talk about a subject in a way that they want to. They can help candidates to talk their way into the job. Open questions also reveal more of the candidates to the interviewers. So interviewers don't rely on 'gut feelings' but base their decisions on actual evidence from the candidates.

Negative questions

The interviewers' questions affect their judgements and final decisions. Questions are sometimes used to reinforce impressions and prejudices. Questions based on negative assumptions about the candidate often only serve to confirm that prejudice. Such questions are often the result of impressions gained from the application form, or from an impression formed as the candidates walked through the door. If interviewers like the candidates, or find they have something in common with them, then they are more likely to ask questions which allow candidates to show themselves in a good light.

The Interview Game

The way questions are asked is as important as what questions are asked. Hypothetical questions often lead to vague answers. Long questions to which the only answer is 'yes' or 'no' make candidates seem inarticulate or lacking in dynamism and motivation. The most damaging type of questions are ones which assume something negative about candidates. Questions like; 'You don't seem to have much experience of. . . ?' or 'Why didn't you. . . ?' Once interviewers have picked up on a negative point from the candidate, they often tend to worry away at it obsessively, and their questions drag the candidates into a downward spiral. Whatever the candidate then says is used by the interviewers to justify their ever more negative impression.

Negative information tends to be regarded as more significant than positive information. Even a small negative point can affect the whole interview, and lose the candidate the chance of the job. Often the questioning is not obviously negative. But persistent questioning about, for example, why the candidate wants to move from their present job, can put candidates on the defensive. It's difficult to show yourself in a positive light when you have to defend your position.

Negative questions tend to irritate candidates. If candidates become exasperated, interviewers' questioning may become cool and distant, and this can aggravate the candidate even more. This dislocation also arises when interviewers, in trying to find out more about the candidate, ask questions in more and more indirect ways. The candidates become less and less clear about what the interviewers want.

Examples

1 An open door

An open question is like an open door. This interviewer invites the candidate to talk about her job in selling.

Interviewer Can you tell me what you were doing at your previous job that would be relevant to this job, bearing in mind there is a lot of contact with the customers in this job?

Candidate Well, I was initially involved in door to door selling. I was selling insurance and goods on credit and that involved meeting people in their own homes. I would collect the money every week and at the same time, introduce them to new products or offers. I got to know them all well, practically as friends, so that they would stay loyal to me.

Interviewer Did you enjoy that line of work?

Candidate I loved it. I did it for five years and in that time I could see my customers build themselves up financially. They stayed with me, they'd say 'We'll see you next week'.

This interviewer has asked an open question, and it leads to a full answer. The second question could just be answered with a 'yes' but the candidate knows that 'yes' would not be enough. Open questions work very successfully provided candidates are helped to relate their answer to the particular job, as in this case. Research has shown that interviews are a more reliable selection procedure when questions are directly related to the most important aspects of the job.

But open questions only work well if interviewers share with candidates an understanding of the purpose of the question and of how much to say.

Learning points

 Candidates and interviewers

Open questions give candidates the opportunity to present themselves in the best possible light.

 Candidates

Recognise open questions as an opportunity to put yourself across as you want to.

 Interviewers

Ask questions that help candidates to talk freely. If they do not talk very much, ask more specific questions.

2 The negative spiral

This interviewer's questions are all loaded against the candidate.

Interviewer I see you've had a fairly mixed bag of jobs over your time, perhaps you could tell me a bit about some of them?

Candidate My last job, if you could call it that, was a company manager negotiating contracts for electrical alarm systems. I also supervised the labour force.

Interviewer What brought you into that particular field? It doesn't seem to tie in with your previous occupation?

Candidate	Well I had to move from my previous job for personal family reasons. I was offered this opportunity and thought I would do well to take it.
Interviewer	I see. Is it family reasons that have often caused you to leave the jobs you've had?

The interviewer's first question is almost certain to put the candidate on the defensive. It implies that the candidate's career has been inconsistent and without direction. And the interviewer's question does not help the candidate to choose what to talk about.

The candidate's answer shows that he feels uncomfortable with the question. The interviewer won't let go. He asks another negative question. And again uses the candidate's answer to confirm his first impression that the man is not career minded and lacks staying power.

Negative questions such as 'What would you say were your weaknesses' are damaging to the candidates and unhelpful to the interviewers.

Learning points

Beware of negative questions. They stifle opportunity and don't help either side.

Turn negative questions around so you can talk about what you can offer that is positive.

Check that your questions are not loaded against the candidate. Don't let questions get into a negative spiral. Help candidates to say what they can offer your organisation. The interview should be an opportunity for the candidates, not a trap.

If the interview is not running smoothly, ask yourself whether it is your own questioning that is preventing the candidate from performing well.

3 The long and the short

Long questions lead to short answers.

Interviewer Are there any particular problems that you have at home in respect of working hours? Do you have to be – do you have any commitments that would affect any particular type of working hours? I'm thinking in particular of certainly on the caretaking side there . . . certain of the positions which involve shifts – different starting and different finishing times – are there any problems there that could be presented?

Candidate No I don't think – No, no problems that I can see.

Interviewers' questions tend to get longer and longer for several reasons. They may feel uncomfortable or embarrassed about the topic. Or they may be trying to set up a hypothetical situation which candidates can relate to. Long, roundabout questions occur most frequently when candidates have contributed very little. Interviewers often assume either that candidates are not forthcoming or that they don't understand the question.

So the interviewers talk more and more as they phrase and rephrase questions, or inject more examples or comments into their questions. The result is that candidates find they have even less chance to talk their way back into the job. It is ironical that the interviewers' intention – to encourage the candidate to speak more – produces precisely the opposite effect. This is a familiar pattern in interviews that are not going well.

Interviewers' long, rambling questions are difficult for the candidate in two other ways. Very often the interviewers' use of language becomes confused because of false starts and oddly constructed sentences. It is hard to pick out the main point and judge the relevance of the rest of the interviewers' talk. In addition, if interviewers think the candidate does not understand them, they will continually rephrase questions in increasingly obvious ways. Candidates then feel they are being talked down to.

Learning points

Remember that the candidates should do most of the talking, not the interviewer.

Give more than yes/no answers so interviewers do not feel they have to fill up the time with long questions.

Ask short questions and don't ask multiple questions.

If there are pauses allow candidates more time or ask another short question to encourage them to talk more.

Don't assume that candidates feel uncomfortable about pauses. Don't rush in to fill the gap.

4 Warning off

This interviewer is uncertain about the candidate's suitability for the job.

Interviewer   There is just one small thing I would like to mention. At this present time we are not in a position to guarantee you a permanent post. I'm not trying to put you off joining us, but if you were to join us, and didn't come up to standard on the training course then we would not be able to keep you on, and it would be back to unemployment for you. How do you feel about that?

If interviewers are doubtful about a candidate's suitability, they often switch from asking questions to warning candidates off the job. In this example, the interviewer spent quite a large part of the interview telling the candidate about the risks of joining the organisation. There is very little candidates can say when they are being put off a job. All they can do is give assurances that they have thought about the risks.

Another way of warning candidates off the job is to explain in detail the worst aspects of the job. For example an interviewer might ask if a candidate could cope with working outside in all weathers. This pattern of questioning often occurs when interviewers have a negative stereotype about candidates because of their sex, ethnic background or age. It can then lead to a negative spiral of questions which confirms the interviewers' image of the candidate.

Learning points

Don't let the interview become a warning off, or a checking up session.

If interviewers stop questioning and start warning, show them from your past experience that you can cope with difficulties.

Don't make candidates feel doubtful about the job just because you feel doubtful about them. Explore other areas which may reveal the candidates' strengths.

8 Coming Across

The outcome of an interview depends on how candidates come across. But how they come across depends on how well both sides communicate together. Everyone has their own style of communicating, of presenting themselves to the world. The way we communicate depends on our background, and is influenced by the people with whom we have close, regular contact.

A nice coincidence

The kind of talk used in interviews is determined by the interviewer's way of communicating and by the conventions of the Interview Game. Since most interviewers are at middle or senior levels of management, the chances are high that they will have brought with them or will have acquired a 'middle class' style of communicating. This usually means that the interviewers will share the same ways of operating in formal settings such as business meetings and interviews. This 'middle class' style coincides precisely with the conventions of the Interview Game. 'Middle class' talk assumes that the hidden meanings behind indirect ways of talking are understood. It assumes that people know what a high premium is put on balanced answers. It assumes that people know how to tailor the truth to fit the expectation that candidates should 'sell' themselves.

Of course many candidates will not share the same style of communicating as interviewers. And the difference in style is often crucial in deciding not to give a candidate the job. 'He wouldn't fit in', 'I wasn't sure what she was getting at', 'I've just a gut feeling that he's not right for the job' are typical remarks when interviewers and candidates have not found a way of communicating well together.

A clash of style

It is not easy for interviewers or anyone else to recognise precisely those differences in style of communications which so affect their final decisions. Everyone has a set of assumptions about what to say and how to talk in any particular situation. These assumptions depend on what we think are the purposes of the encounter. For example, is the interview supposed to be a test or an opportunity for the candidates to sell themselves? These assumptions also depend on what we think is appropriate behaviour: should we be modest, or should we be forceful?

Our assumptions and the subtle features in our talk, like accents and dialects, vary depending on background and our everyday contacts. We have lots of ways of conveying our feelings and of managing our talk with other people – for example, showing when we are listening, or when the other person can take their turn at speaking. These subtle ways include body language, tone of voice and pausing.

Since interviews are made up entirely of talking and listening, differences in style of communicating are not trivial, but vital. Prejudices can easily and quickly be formed on the basis of how people speak. And differences in assumptions and in managing the talk in an interview often lead to awkward moments and misunderstandings. Candidates who are very suitable for a job may be turned down because of these differences.

Differences in communicating may be interpreted in terms of personality and attitudes. For example, someone who speaks slowly may be judged as slow-witted. Or these differences may be mistakenly seen as difficulties in communicating. For example, someone who does not pick up on the hidden purpose of a question may be judged as having poor English. Unsuccessful candidates might well consider they had been discriminated against, if on paper they were very strong candidates. And perceived discrimination is as damaging as real discrimination.

Examples

1 Sharing an understanding

This interviewer and candidate do not share an understanding of what is an appropriate answer.

Interviewer	What sort of driving experience have you had?
Candidate	I passed my test here – when I came to this country. I don't think I've done anything wrong.
Interviewer	Can you tell us why we should appoint you for this job – what particularly do you have to offer?
Candidate	I'm very much interested in this job and I am sure I can do it very well.

Neither of the interviewer's questions are indirect but the candidate does not give the expected answers, the answers that will help him get the job. This is because he does not share the interviewer's assumptions about the purpose of the questions. In the first example, the candidate interprets the question as a checking-up question and not as an offer to describe his experience. Some candidates' only experience of any kind of interview may have been of encounters with officials, which may have been more like interrogations. It may be hard for such candidates to distinguish between the purpose of questions in an interrogation and the purpose of open questions in job interviews.

In his second answer, the candidate says he is interested and can do the job well. But he does not demonstrate this by directly relating his skills and experience to this particular job. Some candidates may not feel they have to sell themselves or may not be aware that interviewers are looking for very particular qualities.

Learning points

Make sure you agree on the purpose of the interview. The purpose is not to try to trick candidates or find them out.

Don't rely on general statements about why you should be offered the job. Be specific about what you, personally, can offer.

Don't assume candidates know that it isn't enough to say they are interested and capable, but that they have to prove it.

2 What do you want me to say?

This interviewer wants to find out the scope and responsibilities of the candidate's previous job.

Interviewer	Can you tell me what your job as a spinner involved?
Candidate A	(pause)
Interviewer	You see, I don't know much about spinning.

Candidate A	Well, first the cotton goes to spinning, then it goes to winding, and then after to twisting. Then it goes to the weaving shed and the cloth is made.
Interviewer	Yes. What did your job as a spinner actually involve?
Candidate A	(long pause)

In this interview the candidate is at a loss, he does not know what the interviewer wants him to say. Asking what is involved in a job assumes a lot of shared knowledge. It assumes that people know they are being asked to describe their particular job at a certain level of detail and with reference to specific skills and abilities. As in this next interview for an engineering job . . .

| *Interviewer* | Can you tell me what your job involved? |
| *Candidate B* | It was maintaining and looking after the machinery so that if any faults cropped up you just did a quick repair to keep them on the move. |

This candidate knows what the interviewer is looking for, so he knows what to say and how much to say. He knows what will make his answer sound relevant. He knows that his answer must be about what he does personally, not a general description of the operation.

What the candidates say and how much they say is also important at the end of the interview, when they are invited to ask their own questions. A candidate's motivation is often judged by whether they do ask questions at that point, and what they ask about.

Learning points

Make sure both sides agree on what the question is trying to find out.

Ask for clarification if you are not sure how you are expected to answer questions.

Don't assume even apparently straightforward questions are easy to answer. Make the purpose of each question clear.

3 Getting your point across

This interview is for the job of supervisor. The interviewer uses an indirect question to try to find out how the candidate would deal with absenteeism.

Interviewer   Now as a supervisor you'll have to deal with absenteeism. What are your feelings about workers who seem to be off sick with this or that wrong with them?

Candidate   Well, where I am now we all get along well together, we know about each other. And as far as I'm concerned that's not been a problem for me. But there are one or two lads who have bad backs – it seems like a lot of the time. Maybe they abuse the system. But I know one man who has a lot of genuine sickness and, because of the others, it reflects on him as well.

The candidate's initial response does not seem to be answering the question. This is partly because the interviewer's question is indirect. The candidate does not know whether the interviewer is indirectly checking up on his own absenteeism rate, or is interested in the candidate's views generally on how to tackle absenteeism. The answer also seems to lack any immediate relevance because the candidate has a style of communicating which means he describes his general situation first, and then makes his main point. In fact, he does eventually answer the question but he does it in his own terms, not the interviewer's.

Learning points

There is more than one way of making a point.

To help the interviewer, relate your answer as directly as you can to the question.

Hear the candidates out. Don't switch off because what they say does not at first seem to be relevant. Important points may come at the end.

4 Interview talk

A chargehand in an engineering company is being interviewed for the post of foreman.

> *Interviewer* What satisfaction will you get from being a foreman?
>
> *Candidate* If I'm, if I knew that I am capable of doing that job as a foreman, I would be quite satisfied if . . . er . . . the day to day operations went the way how I wanted them to . . . If I was I wouldn't have applied for a foreman's job. Then it would have given me satisfaction,

that this is how my ability has been put into the line.

The same chargehand now talking to a production manager on the shop floor:

Chargehand The valve which we sent for repair a couple of weeks ago, they haven't sent it back. The reason they haven't delivered it is the prices they quoted suddenly have gone up by 60%.

If he is to become a foreman, the chargehand needs to be able to talk about the everyday problems on the production line, as in the second example. But his suitability for the job is judged on how well he answers interview questions, as in the first example. So he is judged on how well he talks in the formal interview, for quite another situation – managing on the shop floor. It is clearly much more difficult to answer the abstract and indirect question in the interview (when the candidate is under stress) than it is to explain something factual in familiar circumstances. It is not surprising that the candidate's answer in the interview seems far less clear and precise than his explanation on the shop floor.

On the basis of his interview answer he might be judged as not being a good communicator, or not being a very clear-headed or forceful person. But in the real situation on the shop floor his communication skills would no doubt be rated highly. So this perfectly suitable candidate might easily be turned down.

Learning points

Talking well at interview only proves that candidates can talk well in interviews. It does not prove how well they would communicate in a job.

Prepare for the fact that many questions in interviews will be abstract and indirect, and that you will be talking under stress to people you do not know.

Don't assume that candidates who talk well in an interview will communicate well in the job. And don't assume that candidates who don't talk well in an interview will not be able to communicate well in the job.

PART TWO

TRAINING
ISSUES

---

1 Introduction

1.1 The scope of Part Two

This part of the book is for trainers, organisers and advisers who are responsible for setting up selection interview training. It may also be of interest to those working in the field of language and communication. The discussion in this second part of the book concentrates on equal opportunities and interviewing of minority ethnic groups. It does not attempt to include all the issues of selection interviewing. The rationale for this is given in 1.2.

The aim of this part is to give trainers some of the theoretical background and research on which the points in Part One are based. Part Two Chapters 3–8 examines in more detail the points raised in Part One Chapters 3–8. Chapter 9 gives suggestions on how *The Interview Game* BBC television programmes and this book could be used in training sessions.

It is not intended to be a detailed training manual but rather to deepen trainers' understanding of how language and communication are used in an interview. Anyone organising equal opportunities interviewing training is welcome to contact the Industrial Language Training Service which can offer advice and training.[1]

1.2 Why equal opportunities interviewing?

Part Two concentrates on issues related to equal opportunities interviewing, and specifically to the

[1]National Centre for Industrial Language Training, The Havelock Centre, Havelock Road, Southall, Middx.

interviewing of minority ethnic group candidates, for three reasons:

○ There are a number of good books available on selection interviewing in general, but very little on equal opportunities interviewing.

○ Being a good interviewer in a mono-cultural setting does not necessarily mean you will be a good interviewer in a cross-cultural setting.

○ Acquiring the skills and sensitivities for being a good cross-cultural interviewer should make you a skilled and sensitive interviewer with any candidate.

The next three paragraphs look at these points in more detail.

1.3   Selection interviewing
There are a number of books on the general principles and good practice of selection interviewing. The Open University *Personnel Selection and Interviewing Course* (p. 673) provides an excellent summary. There are also several standard texts such as John Munro Fraser's *Employment Interviewing* (1978), Alec Rodger's *Seven Point Plan* (1974) and Michael Argyle's *The Social Psychology of Work* (1974). Tiffin and McCormick's *Industrial Psychology and Selection* (1975) and *Assessment at Work* by Gilbert and Helen Jessup (1975) are particularly interesting on the kind of talking that should go on in an interview.

There has also been a great deal of research done on employment interviewing. It makes rather dismal reading since the great bulk of the research finding suggests that interviews are unreliable methods of selection. On the brighter side, the research shows that structured interviews are more reliable than unstructured ones. The most comprehensive review of research is by Arvey and Campion (1982) in the journal *Personnel Psychology: The Employment Interview: A Summary and Review of Recent Research.*

However, none of the above material tackles issues of equal opportunities interviewing as its central theme. There is a great deal of literature on racial discrimination in employment which includes discussion on unfair practices in recruitment and selection. These include the Commission for Racial Equality's publications:— *Code of Practice: For the Elimination of Racial Discrimination and the Promotion of Equality of Opportunity in Employment* (1984) and a series of guides on implementing Equal Opportunity in Employment. The T.U.C., the C.B.I. and the Institute of Personnel Management have also published guides. David Wainwright's *Discrimination in Employment* and *Learning from Uncle Sam: Equal Opportunities Programmes* are also useful. Employment practice in Local Authorities has been well researched by Young and Connelly (1982) in the Policy Studies Institute publications.

There is also some work on selection testing, notably by Michael Pearn (1981) *The Fair Use of Selection Tests.* These materials give guidance on procedures and on questions relating to the law. But they were not written to provide detailed help on how to question, listen, interpret, and make judgements in cross cultural interviews.

1.4 Mono-cultural and cross-cultural interviews

The facts of racial discrimination speak for themselves. Despite the efforts of race relations organisations, the level of discrimination and disadvantage in employment has not been significantly reduced (Colin Brown 1984). There are clearly many deep-seated structural reasons for this lack of progress. But one readily identifiable reason is the way in which the selection interview tends to discriminate against minority ethnic groups.

The job interview is one of the most culture-specific events in public life. The title of the BBC series *The Interview Game* was chosen because interviews, like games, are full of conventions and rules which are only known or acquired by a relatively small proportion of the population. Just how culture-specific the job interview is only becomes apparent when those who do not know the rules are required to play the game. Interviewers often assume the candidate was inadequate. But a close analysis of such interviews and post-interview discussions reveals that it is the interview itself which is poorly conducted.

Such analysis comes as a shock to many interviewers who consider they are skilled and experienced, and express considerable good will towards black candidates. But good will and skills for a mono-cultural setting are not enough. Much of the guidance suggested in standard texts is unhelpful and even counterproductive in cross-cultural settings. For example, advice is given in Tiffin and McCormick, and in Jessup and Jessup which is useful where interviewers and candidates share the same style of communicating, but would be confusing in a cross-cultural interview. For example, Jessup and Jessup suggest that if you want the candidate to talk more you should not leave long pauses and you should make encouraging noises. But candidates with a different style of communicating may not interpret these signals as the invitation to add to what they have said.

1.5 Skills and sensitivities

The conventions of the traditional British interview can put minority ethnic groups at a particular disadvantage. This type of interview can also disadvantage anyone who does not fit the stereotype of the conventional candidate.

It is hoped, therefore, that raising awareness of how judgements of black candidates are made by white interviewers will help all interviewers to:

○ Check their own assumptions before judging others.

○ Be explicit about the purpose of the whole interview and of particular questions.

○ Monitor their own behaviour to ensure that they are not reacting rigidly.

○ Accept a wide variety of styles of communicating.

If interviewers do not monitor and adjust their behaviour to become more flexible communicators, they may simply choose the candidates most like themselves. The traditional interview tends to do just this. It is a cautious and conservative procedure. Good, but unconventional, candidates are not selected, and organisations always appoint the same kind of people. They do not, therefore, benefit from the changes that less conventional candidates could effect in these organisations.

2 Communication and Discrimination

Black people continue to face discrimination when employers select and promote staff. The introduction of equal opportunity policies has not produced fundamental changes in employment practice. Discrimination has still to be tackled at the point at which decisions are made about individuals. It is possible to document the processes which lead to a form of indirect discrimination by examining how judgements are made as people communicate in interviews and by relating these to the records and statistics known about discrimination.

2.1 The role of communication in indirect discrimination

The approach in *The Interview Game* is based on the work of John Gumperz at the University of California and the Industrial Language Training Service (I.L.T.) in Britain. Since 1976 John Gumperz and his research team and I.L.T. have worked collaboratively on research and training in cross-cultural communication.

This approach has developed from individual case studies of inter-ethnic encounters, to the analysis of a wider data base of inter-ethnic and intra-ethnic interviews. It has also been deepened by the experiences and perceptions of black and white trainers. It has, therefore, been possible to examine the interpretative processes which take place in cross-cultural communication and relate these to the wider social issues of disadvantage and discrimination.

The basis for this co-operation is described in *Crosstalk* (1979) published by the National Centre for Industrial Language Training.[1] This book does not include the theoretical background or practical training issues which led to the making of the BBC TV programme *Crosstalk*. Readers are advised to obtain a copy of the *Crosstalk* booklet and accompanying notes Gumperz, Jupp and Roberts (1979, 1981).

The dimension of communication in discrimination has often been misunderstood. It is seen as a cover-up or excuse for 'real' discrimination. However, research and experience indicate that communication can be a major factor. The way in which communication works as a form of indirect discrimination is largely a hidden process (Gumperz 1982b). This hidden process is the result of a negative cycle in which the low social position of black people in Britain, racism, discrimination and communication differences all operate to reinforce each other. The detailed examination of interactions between blacks and whites, whose style of communicating is not shared, often shows that the interactions have confirmed existing negative impressions of the other group. These negative impressions are then incorporated into the structured experience of that group and become part of the stored knowledge that individuals take to their next encounter. The white official assumes the black person will not be suitable. The black applicant expects to be discriminated against.

---

[1] The film and booklet examine some of the ways in which negative group stereotypes can be created and reinforced as a result of culturally specific uses of English. Examples are taken from native English speakers and North Indian English speakers.

People often think of the term 'communication' in a narrow way, but in the term 'communication' we include here four levels of communication:

Level 1   The prior knowledge which people bring to an encounter to make sense of it. This stored knowledge or 'schema' sets up what Deborah Tannen (1979b) has called 'structures of expectation' which are brought to every encounter.

Level 2   The processes of interpretation and inferencing which the listener uses all the time to interpret the speaker's intention.

Level 3   The management or co-ordination of talk: knowing when to take a turn, knowing how long to talk, knowing how to make a contribution seem relevant.

Level 4   Means of expression: grammar, vocabularly, intonation and rhythm of speech.

So at Level 1 there are general expectations and attitudes and at the Level 4 there are subtle, momentary and usually unconscious signals of talk. For example, awkward moments that arise from long pauses or interruptions (Level 3) can reinforce negative ethnic stereotypes (Level 1). Or, differing notions about what is expected in an interview (Level 1) are never resolved because neither side picks up from the other the subtle cues which signal that they are at cross-purposes (Levels 2 and 4).

This expanded view of communication, therefore, includes the beliefs and value judgements that are brought to the interview. For a black candidate these are likely to include experience of discrimination, and a particular set of expectations about the interview. They will also include a store of interactional knowledge which determines, for example, how direct to be or which subjects are taboo. For a white interviewer, this stored knowledge will probably include the value system of the institution they represent, rather different expectations about the interview and different interactional knowledge.

Relating this expanded view of communication to decision making in formal settings, the bald facts of institutionalised discrimination can be connected with individual attitudes and behaviour. Individuals can be made aware that even with good will and good intentions, discrimination can still take place. Once people have understood how communication, in its widest sense, affects decisions, they will realise how decisions that seem reasonable and neutral are, in fact, indirectly discriminatory.

2.2 Gatekeeping

In recent years I.L.T. and John Gumperz have concentrated on what have been called 'gatekeeping' interviews. 'Gatekeepers' is a term used by Frederick Erikson and Jeffrey Shultz (1982) to describe those officials in institutions who have control over certain resources, facilities and opportunities, and who decide who should be allowed to have them, who should be allowed through 'the gate'. They include, for example, housing officers, social security clerks, teachers and any of the people who are involved in selection interviewing. Some gatekeepers take for granted that the way they interview candidates and make decisions about them is the right and only way. They assume that if everyone is given the same treatment, then everyone will be treated fairly. Other gatekeepers express concern and good will. They feel uncertain about the judgements they make in many cross-cultural interviews. They are committed to equal opportunities but do not know how to reconcile their committment with their feelings of uncertainty when they interview black candidates.

2.3 Training

For both groups of gatekeepers the purpose of training in equal opportunities interviewing is to help people re-assess how they make judgements about candidates who may not conform to their expectations of good performance in interviews. Part of this process is to help interviewers recognise how culture-specific interviews are. It has taken the presence of black people in Britain to make the white majority realise how conventionalised, and by implication, how absurd are questions such as 'What does your job involve?' or 'Why do you want this job?' These questions arise from a particular 'schema' about how interviews should be conducted.

Interviewers also need to be helped to understand how linguistic and non-verbal cues are used to make talk between people meaningful. Most interviewing training emphasises objectivity and the importance of eliciting enough information from the candidate. But the overt message or content is only part of what constitutes communication. With every message there is a metamessage. In other words, we simultaneously talk and say something about the talk. We convey our attitudes, we show how what we say fits in with the conversation, we indicate our intention without making it explicit. We use our own and other people's metamessages all the time to monitor what is going on and to integrate these findings without expectations. People are constantly making inferences and evaluating (Gumperz 1982/b). Judgements are made as a result of inferencing and evaluating: 'I'd appoint her – she seems dynamic', 'He wouldn't fit somehow', 'I had a few doubts about her motivation'.

Interviewing training helps interviewers to examine the processes involved in communicating in interviews. They can be helped to see that the four levels of communication, defined in 2.1 above, are all interacting on each other all the time.

Another important aspect of communication is the way in which talk between people is jointly negotiated. Whether a conversation or interview goes well depends on how *both* sides involve themselves in the encounter. Interviewers play an active part, both consciously and unconsciously, in constructing the impression the candidate makes on them. If interviewers take positive steps to make the interview a genuine interaction they will help candidates to come across as they want to. It is part of the interviewers' responsibility to help candidates to do this.

Conclusion

Interviewers on training courses can be helped to analyse interviews at these four levels and relate this analysis to both their own experiences and the experiences of black people. Interviewers can then be made more aware of how candidates' responses are typically interpreted and how other interpretations are equally possible and valid. They can also develop new skills. For example, they can learn to make the purpose of their questions explicit, learn to clarify responses themselves and encourage clarification from the candidates. Above all, they can be helped to monitor their own behaviour, to locate their judgements in evidence taken from the interview and to check that they are not assessing the evidence exclusively from their own cultural norms and expectations. The aim of the training is not to teach interviewers how to talk to a particular ethnic group. But the aim is to develop 'communicative flexibility'. This flexibility emerges when interviewers adjust their own communicative styles to take account of communication differences, and when interviewers question their criteria for judging the adequacy of the candidates' performance.

Communicative flexibility develops over time as interviewers become increasingly aware of how they make judgements. As they become more accepting of the notion and more confident in their flexibility, they can 'open the gate' to those who have so often found it shut.

3 First Impressions

Key points in Part One

The way an interview begins can affect the emotional tone and balance of the interview and so its outcome. Research has shown that interviewers typically reach a final decision about the candidate within the first four minutes (Springbett 1958). If that decision is negative then a great deal of time may be spent on checking up on candidates, concentrating on negative aspects or warning them off the job.

It is important that interviewers:

○ Make sure their opening statements and explanations are clear and explicit.

○ Check that candidates know which stages of the interview are meant to relax them.

○ Agree with candidates on the purpose of talking about qualifications.

○ Are aware of the dangers of making stereotypical judgements and guard against using questions to reinforce stereotypes.

3.1 Opening statements and explanations

It is now quite common practice for interviewers to explain to candidates the overall structure of the interview. However, this practice may not be as helpful as it appears, if there is no shared understanding of the purpose of the interview. Candidates who are not familiar with the culture of the interview may have quite different expectations from the interviewer. For example:

Interviewers' expectations The candidates should . . .	Candidates' expectations The candidates should . . .
Sell themselves.	Give correct answers in a test of knowledge.
Establish 'rapport' and a relationship.	Give factual information.
Reveal attitudes and opinions.	Talk in an impersonal way.
Talk freely.	Talk as little as possible so as not to be caught out.

If there are different expectations, interviewers need to be explicit about the purpose of the interview in their opening statement.

Interviewers also need to monitor their description of the job and the organisation. Training can help interviewers to cut out jargon and make their descriptions more precise (Sayers 1983).

3.2 Relaxing the candidate
The most typical questions are about the journey to the interview, and they can help to relax some candidates. But for candidates who do not consider that an interview is about establishing rapport, such questions may appear irrelevant or bizarre. Or the candidates may interpret them as part of the interview 'test' and be worried about how to answer them.

3.3 Qualifications
In many interviews questions about qualifications are dealt with at the beginning in a routine way. These questions are often seen by interviewers as a way of easing the candidate into the interview since the

information is already given in the application form. Besides, the typical attitude of white British people towards qualifications is that they are less important than experience and simply show that you have got the minimum that is required of the job. Minority ethnic candidates may have a very different perception. For example, in the Indian sub-continent, qualifications are considered to demonstrate a good deal about one's personal development and attitudes and therefore are often discussed at length at interviews. Because qualifications say so much about the candidate, an Asian[1] candidate might well answer a question like 'Tell us why we should offer you the job' with a response such as 'Well, I've got the qualifications for the job'. Because of this convention about qualifications in the Indian sub-continent, many Asian candidates may feel able to 'sell' themselves by talking about their qualifications. But they would feel extremely uncomfortable about selling themselves by talking about their experience, their motivation or their opinions.

3.4 Stereotyping

Research shows that pre-interview information, for example from application forms, can often determine post interview decisions (Dipboye 1980). Interviewers also, inevitably, make judgements about candidates as they walk through the door. Their judgements are related to stereotypes of the ideal job candidate (Schmitt 1976). Such stereotyping does not help either interviewers or candidates. But in equal opportunities interviewing, it is essential to tackle negative ethnic stereotyping. Everyone is aware of ethnic stereotypes – even interviewers with good will. Candidates' ethnic

[1]'Asian' is used in this book to describe people from the Indian sub-continent and those whose origins are in the Indian sub-continent but who have come from East Africa.

background is often obvious from their application forms and their appearance. Once this is known, interviewers all too easily make generalisations about their interests, physical capability, and even personal qualities. Questions are then formulated to confirm assumptions and deny candidates the opportunity to present themselves as they really are.

4 Experience Talks

Key points
Candidates' experience cannot itself be assessed at an interview. It is what they say about experience which is assessed. There are conventions about how to talk about experience:

1 Answers should be directly related to the job on offer and should be a mix of fact, opinion and attitudes.
2 It is accepted that candidates should be honest about facts but can tailor the truth so as not to give a bad impression.

Interviewers also have assumptions about:

3 What constitutes a good work record.
4 How hypothetical questions should be answered.

4.1 Relating the answer to the job and giving a mix of fact, opinion and attitude
Apparently straightforward questions like 'What does your job involve?' are extremely difficult to answer if candidates do not share assumptions about what is a relevant answer. In addition, questions about experience are not simply fact-finding. They are intended to elicit evidence of the candidates' motivation, capabilities and personal qualities such as leadership qualities, steadiness and ability to work independently. Analysis

of job interview transcriptions reveals a pattern of questions and answers which maintains the balance between fact, opinion and feelings. Questions such as 'What did you feel about. . . ?', 'Did you enjoy. . . ?' expect an answer in which the candidate's statement of feelings are backed up with reasons. Similarly, 'fact-finding' questions of the type 'Tell me about your time with . . .' are aimed at discovering not only what candidates did but what they felt about what they did.

Candidates who answer questions about feelings with the response 'I felt quite good' or answer factual questions with only impersonal information may be doing so for two reasons. Firstly, they may answer the question at face value, responding to the surface message only. Secondly, their assumptions or 'schema' about the purpose of the interview may lead them to give an unexpected answer. John Gumperz's research on ethnic differences in counselling interviews suggests that in Asian-Asian counselling interviews, the counsellor does a great deal of inferring of fact and opinion, and then checks with the client. Whereas in white British interviews the clients make a lot of evaluative comments about their situation without much prompting from the counsellor. So, there may be quite different cultural assumptions about how evaluative to be in a formal interview.

4.2 Tailoring the truth

By any standard, the highly conventionalised routine of the job interview makes it a peculiar and unnatural event. One of its most disturbing conventions is what we might call the 'stylised honesty' expected of candidates. This takes many forms. For example, it is acceptable for candidates to show they are good at their jobs but not simply to say they are good. In research carried out by Valerie Yates and Clarice Brierley of the Industrial Language Training Service for the Commission for Racial Equality (1984) this convention proved to be very significant. In simulated promotion interviews, white candidates were more likely to demonstrate their attributes by example than black candidates (1983).

Candidates should not state baldly that they are good or have some particular attribute, but are expected to mitigate the statement with 'I think . . .' or other softening phrases. If candidates' work record seems patchy or unconvincing, then they are expected to massage the negative facts into something more positive. For example, candidates who have been unemployed for six months might say they had done 'Nothing' during that time. To the candidates this would be a perfectly reasonable and honest answer. But it would not be considered an adequate answer by interviewers. If interviewers want to hear something positive then they need to be explicit about what they are looking for.

4.3 Work record

For many candidates who do not share the 'white middle-class' culture of the job interview, their responses to questions about work history may lead to misjudgements. Questions about work history, as well as covering the type of work and reasons for changing jobs, also cover job satisfaction and preference. Many minority ethnic group candidates born overseas took jobs where there were gaps in the British labour market and were unable to get work that reflected or took into account their qualifications and experience (Gumperz 1982b). However, interviewers often assume that it is the candidates' personal failings which have prevented them from obtaining appropriate work, and candidates find themselves having to defend a situation which arose because of structural factors related to employment and discrimination. The candidate in the BBC television programme *Crosstalk* is in this position (Gumperz, Jupp, Roberts 1979).

Interviewers usually have a set of reasons for changing jobs that they would consider acceptable. In reality, all candidates change jobs for a wide variety of reasons, both career and personal reasons. However, those who are familiar with the Interview Game know that they are expected to present themselves as continually pushing their career forwards. Minority ethnic candidates who may be less familiar with the hidden conventions of selection interviews, may be more open about their real reasons for changing jobs. They may also, because of their own and their community's situation in Britain have different priorities in seeking and changing jobs.

Finally, factors of job satisfaction and job preference may not be considered at all. Sarah Greenwood's work with Job Centre staff shows that when the staff asked'an Asian work seeker what job he/she would like to do, the answer is frequently 'Any job', followed by a list of previous jobs and skills showing what they can do, but with no preference stated' (Greenwood 1984).

Given the discrimination faced by Asian workers when seeking employment, it is hardly surprising that likes and preferences are perceived as irrelevant luxuries.

4.4 Hypothetical questions
On most interviewing training courses, interviewers are encouraged to avoid using hypothetical questions. Yet, they still remain one of the most common types of questioning in interviews.

Hypothetical questions are difficult for all candidates to answer for the obvious reason that they have to guess how they might react in a situation they do not know, but the interviewers do. These questions are likely to be even more damaging for minority ethnic group candidates. First of all, their circumstances may mean they have a less obviously appropriate work record than their white counterparts. This fact, combined with interviewers' negative stereotypes about their suitability, leads to a disproportionate number of hypothetical questions. Secondly, such questions put unnecessary linguistic demands on candidates who do not speak English as their mother tongue. For example, talking about hypothetical situations requires speakers to set the imaginary scene and to use conditional tenses. Thirdly, hypothetical questions are often about how candidates would deal with people. These questions are in line with Western concepts about psychology, about how to handle people in organisational settings. They require candidates to explain how they would behave in the context of a range of possible options. Interviewers expect an answer like this:

'Depending on whether x or y was the case I would do . . .'

Candidates who do not know this convention may give a more categorical answer and be judged as being rigid or inflexible.

5 The Hidden Message

Key points in Part One
Coping with contradictions tends to make anyone's style of communicating more indirect. In addition, different ethnic groups do not always have the same assumptions as white native English speakers about how direct to be in different contexts. So the hidden message in interviews relates to:

1 Notions of how direct or indirect to be.
2 The hidden agenda of the interview.
3 The hidden purpose of particular questions.
4 Embarrassment and indirectness in dealing with personal questions.
5 Hidden signals in managing talk.

5.1 Notions of how direct or indirect to be

The way in which individuals present themselves and are evaluated depends crucially on what social anthropologists Penny Brown and Stephen Levinson call 'positive' and 'negative' face. Positive face is the desire to be friendly, to be part of a group, to show solidarity. Negative face is the desire to keep a part of oneself private and respect that desire in other people. Brown and Levinson (1978) distinguish five categories of politeness strategies for positive and negative face ranging from 'bald on record', that is 'Say exactly what you want', to not saying anything at all because the risk of loss of face is too great. In a job interview, as Ron and Suzanne Scollon (1983) point out, interviewer and candidate may have very different perceptions about how much they should be showing positive face and solidarity, or how much negative face and deference.

Candidates who say very little or respond in an impersonal way may well be using what in their minds is the appropriate deference strategy for someone in a position of higher power or status. However, interviewers usually assume that candidates will use 'solidarity' strategies and go out of their way to relate to the interviewers and collaborate with them by sharing opinions and attitudes. Conflicting styles and expectations may cause candidates to be wrongly judged as withdrawn or unmotivated.

5.2 The hidden agenda

Interviewers and candidates may not share assumptions about how candidates should present themselves at interviews. So, at any stage of the interview, both sides may be at cross-purposes: interviewers may be trying to relax the candidate, while the candidate thinks they are being checked up on; candidates may be trying to be modest and unassuming when interviewers expect them to 'sell' themselves. The two sides may have different ways of trying to accomplish their overall goal. Further confusion can arise from the interviewers' line of questioning. Because the whole style of an interview is so indirect and because interviewers control its direction, candidates often don't know where the questioning is leading and whether the interviewer has switched topics.

If any talk is to be collaborative then speakers have to know what the topic is and why it is being talked about at that point. As the conversation analyst Harvey Sacks pointed out (Sacks 1971) there is a continual monitoring in conversation – listeners ask themselves 'Why that now to me?'. However, in interviews, interviewers often switch rapidly from topic to topic without signalling they are doing so, or pursue a line of questioning which keeps the real topic of the questions hidden. As discourse analysts have shown (see, for example, a useful summary of discourse topic in Brown and Yule, 1983) speakers are unlikely to feel comfortable with the conversation if the contributions to it are seen to be irrelevant. In fact relevance is considered by Grice (1975) to be a basic maxim of conversational co-operation. If interviewers are not explicit about the topic, they cannot necessarily expect candidates to speak relevantly to it.

5.3   The hidden purpose of particular questions

The notion of 'schema' has already been introduced. Where interviewers and candidates have different overall schema about the purpose of interviews, the interpretation of the speakers' intent in a particular question may also be wrong. In this example (Roberts and Sayers, in press), the interviewer's intention was to find out about the quality of the candidate's maths:

Interviewer	How's your maths?
Candidate	(Silence)
Interviewer	Not so good, eh?
Candidate	No

The 'schema' in the interviewer's head is that since many candidates do not have paper qualifications and are often embarrassed about their level of maths, indirect questions like 'How's your maths?' are the best way of finding out. The interviewer interprets the candidate's silence as embarrassment about his poor maths. The candidate, feeling he must defer to the interviewer, agrees that his maths is not good. In fact, the candidate, whose mother tongue is not English, is thrown by the question which sounds like 'How's your family' or 'How's your cough?'. In addition, the indirectness of the question hides the interviewer's schema from him, so the purpose of the question remains obscure.

5.4 Dealing with personal questions

Personal or embarrassing questions are often put in an indirect way. In cross-cultural interviews, interviewers may feel embarrassed when trying to find out about quite straightforward matters. This can happen when they feel they have not fully understood what the candidate has said. Their embarrassment leads them to become increasingly indirect in the way they try to ask for clarification or regain control of the interview (Roberts and Sayers, in press).

Interviewers often ask questions concerning race and gender in an indirect way, either because they are embarrassed or because they are worried about contravening the law. The Sex Discrimination Act, 1975, and the Race Relations Act, 1976, have made it illegal to treat someone unfairly because of their gender, marital status, or racial or ethnic background. It is discriminatory to ask questions of some candidates and not others about child care, or about getting on with a particular ethnic group. Trying to get round any legal constraints by indirect questions is still against the spirit of the law. Indirect questions could be used as evidence in an industrial tribunal.

Some candidates may wish to talk openly about discrimination. Certainly the great majority of black candidates will have experienced some form of discrimination or abuse. But interviewers should not assume that candidates will want to discuss such sensitive issues openly.

5.5 Hidden signals in managing talk

The term 'managing talk' includes the ways in which speakers and listeners take turns to talk. (The work of the conversation analysts Sacks, Schegloff and Jefferson (1974) has explored turn-taking in detail.) Two of the most important ways in which speakers know when to take turns are prosody and non-verbal communication. The term 'prosody' includes intonation, pausing, pitch, rhythm, voice quality and stress as perceived by the listener. The non-verbal signals most crucial in managing talk are head and eye movements. In interviews it is vital that interviewers make clear when they want the candidate to go on talking, and when they thinking the candidate has said enough.

A number of books on selection interviewing suggest ways to help the interviewer manage the candidates' talk. For example, in *Selection and Assessment at Work* (1975) Gilbert and Helen Jessup suggest 'making 'encouraging noises' to get candidates to elaborate. To stop candidates talking they suggest interviewers should agree with them and then look away from them. Tiffin and McCormick (1965) recommend pausing to allow candidates to fill the gap, and repeating key responses in a questioning tone (quoted in Greenwood 1984).

However, all these suggestions assume that interviewers and candidates are both employing the turn-taking strategies used by native speakers of English in white British culture. Research on inter-ethnic communication has shown that both prosody and non-verbal communication are highly specific to different ethnic and linguistic groups. Erickson and Shultz have shown that black and white Americans often have different ways of showing they are listening or of offering a turn to the listener (1982). Gumperz, Aulakh and Kaltman have contrasted the use of prosody among native English speakers with the prosody used by speakers of English from an Asian background (Gumperz 1982b). Pausing, rise and falls in pitch levels and intonation are used systematically in different ways by different groups. So, for example, interviewers cannot assume that repeating a word with rising intonation is necessarily interpreted by the candidate as 'an encouraging noise' and an invitation to elaborate. The candidates may well interpret it as a signal that the interviewer has understood and perhaps agrees with what they have said, and they need say no more.

6 Getting On Together

Key points in Part One
It's hardly surprising that research shows that there is a fairly strong relationship between interviewers liking a candidate and their overall positive evaluation (Keenan 1977). Since candidates who get on with interviewers are more likely to get the job, it is important to understand what those aspects of communication are that make interviewers feel comfortable and positive. If interviewers are aware of these aspects they are more likely to take account of them when conducting a fair selection interview. They can take positive action to ensure that those interviewers who do not share a lot with candidates, do not automatically rule them out as unsuitable, or as not 'fitting in'. Awareness raising and positive action are supported by recent research on interviews.

1 Erickson and Shultz's research in counselling interviews is particularly helpful in analysing how communication functions in interviews.
2 Post-interview discussions highlight the difficulties interviewers identify when trying to make interviews more like conversations.

6.1 Communication in counselling interviews

In *The Counsellor as Gatekeeper* (1982) Erickson and Shultz examined a series of inter-ethnic counselling interviews. They found that the overall 'emotional tone' of the interview predicted its likely outcome. This tone was the result of:

1 fixed features such as ethnicity, race and gender.
2 information discovered in the interview such as experience, activities, biographical facts.
3 evaluation of people on the basis of their style of communicating – such as eye contact, listening behaviour and speech rhythms.
4 co-membership – having particular attributes in common, for example, both fixed features (such as ethnicity) and discovered attributes (such as both enjoying the same sport).

The latter two categories are particularly crucial in 'getting on together'. Some aspects of communicative style are not processed consciously at all, such as eye contact and rhythm. For example, lack of rhythmic co-ordination between speakers both indicates and exacerbates uncomfortable moments in the interview. And different uses of eye contact and head movement, to indicate when the listener is listening, can lead to the speaker talking on and on because they assume the listener did not hear or did not understand. Where there is a clash of communicative style, interviewers may attribute their feelings of discomfort to poor candidate performance. They are simply unaware that this clash of style is a feature of poor communication between themselves and the candidates. '. . . the difficulties that ethnically different counsellors and students experienced did not result from any special malevolence on the part of the counsellors, they just happened' (Erickson and Shultz).

Erickson and Shultz also found that co-membership, (sharing membership of a particular group) was the most significant factor in helping counselling interviews go well. There were fewer uncomfortable moments, more offering of advice and less checking up. Interviewers need to be aware of how easy it is for co-membership to affect their judgement of candidates. Conversely, they could take positive action and go out of their way to find points of common interest with those candidates from a different ethnic background, provided, of course, that candidates are aware of and accept these solidarity strategies. They should try to establish something in common with such candidates. But if candidates do not respond easily, then interviewers should not pursue it. It is a strategy that may help some candidates but not all.

6.2 Making interviews more like a conversation

Questioning in interviews can become like an interrogation, especially when adults are asked about their early home background or reasons for coming to Britain. It may remind them, for example, of encounters with immigration officials and they may answer as if indeed the job interview is an interrogation.

One way to make interviews less like interrogations is to give feedback to show that the interviewers are actively listening. Active listening means interviewers showing candidates that what they are saying is heard, interpreted and responded to. It means giving feedback by summing up the candidates' main point or by commenting briefly on what they have said or by asking follow-up questions. It also means checking back if the candidates' contribution does not seem clear.

The Interview Game

It may be even more important to do this when interviewer and candidate do not share the same style of communicating. Post-interview discussions with interviewers show that when they did not fully understand what the candidate said they were often too embarrassed to clarify with the candidate, and simply wrote off what the candidate said as meaningless (Roberts and Sayers, in press). Part of the interviewers' responsibility towards candidates is to make sure they have understood the candidates.

7 The Power of Questions

7.0 Key points in Part One

Since interviewers focus their attention on candidates and their performance, they often fail to notice the effect they are having on the candidates. Yet interviewers' questions shape the image of the candidate that comes across. This is because:

1   The interview is a dynamic process in which both sides are 'partners' in a joint task.
2   The impact of negative questioning is rarely appreciated.
3   Cross-purposes and different styles of talking lead to unproductive and damaging questions.

7.1 The interview as a dynamic process

The interview is an event with certain fixed aspects to it, such as the imbalance of power, the interviewers' control of questioning and a fixed goal. However, the interview is also a dynamic process. As people talk they are constantly creating a new context within which their particular contribution at that time is judged. So decisions about candidates can change from moment to moment. When interviews are not going well, interviewers tend to create a less and less favourable context. The interview is not an objective event with set questions. It is an encounter between people talking together in which highly subjective judgements are made all the time. But since interviewers are in control, they can use their power to ask questions which either change or maintain the context of that particular part of the interview.

7.2 The impact of negative questioning

Summaries of research studies on interviews (Mayfield (1963), Wright (1969) and Schmitt (1976)) all show that negative information is rated as more significant than positive information. Interviewers find reasons for 'knocking-out' candidates. And this witch-hunting for negative factors prevents the interview from being an opportunity for candidates to display their suitability for the post.

This negative attitude towards interviewing can have a disproportionately negative impact on black candidates. There is considerable evidence (McIntosh and Smith, 1974 and Smith 1977) to show that black candidates are discriminated against in interviews. If interviewers are prejudiced against black candidates, then interviewers' style and choice of questions will set up a negative dynamic from which the candidate cannot escape.

7.3 Cross-purposes and different styles of talking

If both sides do not share an understanding of the purpose of questions and have different styles of communicating, the balance between questions and answers can be quickly lost. The ratio of interviewer/candidate talking time should be about 30%:70%. Once there is imbalance, both sides, unconsciously, tend to reinforce it. So, if interviewers ask long questions and get short answers, their discomfort leads to even longer questions and to even shorter answers from candidates. This mutually reinforcing imbalance has been dubbed 'Complementary schismogenesis' by Gregory Bateson. And the notion has been developed by the sociolinguist Deborah Tannen in her work on conversation.

This imbalance in a conversation or interview affects not only the amount of talk but how and in what tone things are talked about. For example, one speaker can become increasingly angry and irritated as the other speaker becomes more and more cool and calm. Once speakers have realised this is happening, they may be able to stop the downward spiral and start again.

One particular imbalance in the amount of talk occurs when interviewers assume candidates have not understood. Either candidates do not appear to be listening to the question, or they give a minimal response. Interviewers then launch into a much longer question to try to elicit the expected full answer. This often leads to a very short answer. So an even longer question is asked. And so on. Erickson calls this phenomenon 'hyper-explanation'. It regularly occurs when a white interviewer fails to pick up a black candidate's listening responses. The increasingly lengthy explanations either confuse candidates or insult them because the candidates feel they are being talked down to.

8 Coming Across

Key points in Part One

Identifying all the different factors that affect how candidates 'come across' is extremely complex. Interviewers will be assessing in their own terms how intelligible the candidate is and the extent to which candidates are relevant and persuasive in what they say.

These three criteria, effectiveness, relevance and intelligibility, depend on:

1 How far both sides share a style of communicating.
2 How much both sides share assumptions about the proper conduct of the interview.
3 How comfortably both sides manage the interaction.
4 How far interviewers have appreciated how different interview talk is from ordinary conversation.

8.1 Sharing a style of communicating

Sharing a style of communicating means sharing a tradition of what is considered appropriate and meaningful to say. People who share such a tradition are said to be members of the same 'speech community'. They not only share the same language, but they share the same way of interpreting the speech and listening behaviour particular to their group. A particular style of communicating identifies people as part of a group. (How communication creates group identity is described in *Language and Social Identity* (1982b) edited by John Gumperz.)

In an unequal encounter like an interview, candidates who do not share a style of communicating with interviewers will be at a disadvantage. They may be categorised as part of a group which triggers negative stereotypes among the interviewers. They may also find misunderstandings or uncomfortable moments occur because each side misinterprets the other's intentions or because they lack shared assumptions about how talk should be managed.

John Gumperz and other sociolinguists have shown that these 'speech communities' are not watertight compartments at all. Many individuals can switch their ways of speaking when the context changes. They may do this consciously or unconsciously. It would be quite wrong to assume that because individuals are from a particular social or ethnic group, that they will always communicate in a way characteristic of that group.

So, while candidates from a particular ethnic group may have a culturally specific style of communicating which is not shared with the interviewers, they may also have a great deal of what John Gumperz has called 'communicative flexibility'. In other words, they may be able to adapt their style, or certain aspects of it, to accord with the interviewers' style.

The outcome of interviews depends both on what is known and assumed before the interview, and what actually goes on in it. Both sides bring to the interview assumptions about the purpose of interviews and about appropriate behaviour. But the outcome also depends on how both sides react to each other during the different stages of the encounter. Culture-specific styles of communicating affect the expectations both sides bring to interviews, and the way the interview is conducted and progressed.

8.2 Assumptions which affect communication

Chapter 3 in Part Two outlined some different expectations about the goals of interviews and how they should be accomplished. These differences determine how far the interview is perceived as a positive and co-operative activity. The sense of well-being which participants have in a conversation when they feel they 'see eye to eye', 'really get on well together', 'feel comfortable together' is directly related to how co-operative the talk is.

The philosopher Paul Grice (1975) has proposed four maxims of conversational co-operation: you must say enough but not too much, you must be truthful, you must be relevant and you must be clear. What individuals consider 'co-operative' depends upon their traditions of communicating. So, for example, knowing how much to say in answer to an interview question will depend upon candidates' view of what is the right amount. The maxim of truth is hard to follow in an interview because the convention of the interview is that the candidate should not be so honest as to give a bad impression. The maxim of relevance depends on understanding the hidden message of questions. And this in turn depends upon the kind of stored experiences candidates bring to interviews and their knowledge of interview conventions. For many black candidates, past experience with white officials means that they interpret fact-finding questions as questions to 'catch them out'. Their answers might appear defensive to the interviewers who were expecting a purely factual answer.

A question like 'What does your job involve?' is also difficult to answer without knowing the interview conventions and some candidates may consider it an absurd question. To answer it relevantly the candidates must know that the preferred answer should be a few utterances long, should indicate your range of responsibilities and take account of what interviewers are likely to know about the work.

8.3   Managing the talk
Managing the interview comfortably will depend upon how the flow of talk is managed and how clearly and intelligibly the two sides come across to each other.

Conversation analysts have shown how much interactional work goes on at a non-verbal level to manage the flow of talk (in particular the work of Harvey Sacks and Gail Jefferson). In smoothly managed interaction, both sides pick up unconsciously subtle cues which indicate when it is their turn to speak and whether the other is listening. These cues act as a kind of monitor to check that the conversation is proceeding collaboratively. Erickson and Shultz have found that smooth conversations develop a rhythm which both sides naturally fall into. When participants do not share a communicative style, they tend to find it more difficult to maintain this comforting rhythmic pattern. Awkward moments in interviews are often characterised by a lack of co-ordinated rhythm. Interviewers have a vague feeling of discomfort but do not know why. They start to believe the candidate won't 'fit in' and cannot locate their unease in incompatible styles of communicating.

Making points clearly is particularly difficult in the formal, decontextualised setting of the interview (see 8.4). If people feel uncomfortable in an interview, they are less likely to ask for clarification.

Interviewers may judge candidates as lacking clarity in their line of argument for three main reasons. Firstly, as we have already suggested, if candidates do not know the purpose of the question they may introduce points which are perceived as irrelevant. Secondly, they may order and emphasise their points in a way that is unfamiliar to the interviewers. For example, some candidates use a narrative style in which the argument is gradually built up through description and context. (There are a number of interesting case studies of different styles in Gumperz 1982, Kochman 1974, and Heath 1983.) Thirdly, there can be information loss on both sides if interviewers and candidates do not use prosodic features in the same way.

John Gumperz and his colleagues (Gumperz 1982a & b) have examined some of the systematic differences which occur between speakers of the standard variety of English and Asian bi-lingual speakers who do not speak the standard variety. The BBC TV programme *Crosstalk* explained how some of this information loss can occur. In particular *Crosstalk* examines the influence of North Indian languages on the way intonation, pitch and rhythm are used by Asian bi-lingual speakers of English. In an inter-ethnic exchange differences in the use of these features can mean that both sides may have difficulty in working out the connection between what has just been said and what is being said now. They may also have difficulty in picking up points of contrast and emphasis. Different uses of prosody may complicate matters where there are also grammatical or lexical confusions. It is not uncommon for people to understand 'every word' and yet not make sense of what the speaker said. In other words, the function of prosody to convey meaning, although rarely understood, is crucial to communication.

8.4 Interview talk

In an interview the context of communication is different from a conversation or everyday workplace talk. Roles and relationships, purpose of talk and physical setting are all different in an interview. Roles and relationships are clearly defined and will be unequal and formal. Whereas the purpose of workplace talk is usually to get things done, by contrast the purpose of the interview is for candidates to display themselves through talk.

Communication is more abstract in the interview because an interview is an environment created by talk and not an environment in which talk merely contributes to the activities going on. Experience and behaviour have to be referred to or hypothesised about. And since the setting is not the physical setting of the workplace, all the usual people and objects that can be used to make communication easier, are missing.

This context puts enormous linguistic demands on all candidates. Demands which may be quite unrealistic in terms of the job on offer. Candidates need to be able to use complex grammatical structures, to make reference to people, place and time in what may be long explanations and descriptions, while at the same time they need to keep 'tuned in' to the interviewers' verbal and non-verbal responses. In addition, much of the linguistic currency of an interview is abstract terms such as 'respect', 'capability' and 'interest'. And different cultural groups may well bring different meanings to these words.

Few employers have considered systematically whether the communication skills required by the interview are the same as those of the job. Where this analysis has been done in relation to shopfloor jobs as in the research on promotion interviews referred to in 4.2 the evidence is overwhelming that interviews demand communication skills which are not required for the job. And they do not necessarily assess those skills which are required for the job.

Conclusion

It is difficult to make out a case for continuing to use interviews when they seem to have so little to recommend them. But they are being used more than ever and since they are still crucial in people's life chances, they could at least be run more fairly and effectively. Here are a few pointers:

i   Provide training in equal opportunities interviewing.

ii If there are likely to be black candidates, ensure that there will be black interviewers on the panel, or at least a black person observing.

iii Establish how far the type of communication skills required for the interview are necessary for the job. For jobs which do not require the communication skills demanded in interviews use more direct methods of assessing candidates. For example, studies on the reliability of Assessment Centres suggest they are a more accurate method of selection than the selection interview.

9 Using
The Interview Game
in Training

This chapter's aim is to give some suggestions on how the BBC television series *The Interview Game* could be included in different types of training.[1] The background of the making of the series and a brief description of its contents are also given.

9.1 *The Interview Game*

The Interview Game is a series of five programmes about the talking that goes on in 'gatekeeping' interviews. The purpose of the series is to show how important this talking is if applicants are to get jobs, advice or access to scarce resources such as housing. The five programmes are:

1 The selection interview
2 Training for selection interviews
3 The housing interview
4 The health interview
5 Body language

This book and the suggestions for training are concerned only with programmes 1 and 2 which are about selection interviewing. Programmes 3 and 4 will be useful for those working in housing and the health and social services. Programme 5 examines an aspect of communication in all interviews and will be useful for groups undertaking all kinds of interviewing training.

[1]Video recording: the recording of BBC Education programmes is permitted under certain circumstances. For details of the copyright regulations please write to BBC Villiers House, London W5 2PA.

The Interview Game

For programmes 1, 3 and 4, the BBC was given permission to film the job, housing and health interviews as they actually occurred. Applicants, clients and patients who were waiting to be interviewed were asked if they were willing to be filmed. Only those who agreed were filmed. There was no prior selection of particularly suitable interviewees. The programmes, therefore, represent what actually happened.

It was important to use naturally occurring material in the programmes. Equal opportunities interviewing is a very sensitive subject which challenges the way interviewers make judgements about people. In training courses, it is easy for participants to become uncomfortable and, as a defence mechanism, start to criticise the training material. It is common for role-played or constructed interviews to be criticised as exaggerated, or set-up to make a particular training point.

It is possible that participants on training courses will criticise the interviews in these programmes on other grounds. They may say that the interviews in their institution are conducted differently or are more effective. Obviously, there will be differences between different institutions. And at one level, every single interview is unique. However, the data base of videoed interviews held at the National Centre for Industrial Language Training, collected over the last seven years, shows that the encounters in the BBC programmes are typical of interviews taking place every day.

9.2 *The Interview Game*: Programme 1

Programme outline
The programme starts with an introduction to the series. There are brief examples of medical and housing interviews. The job selection process at London Transport is described. The programme is then divided under

four main headings: *Experience, Questions, Contact* and *Answers*.

Suggestions for use of a video recording in training
The video should not be shown without preparation (see 9.4 below), nor should it be shown straight through without stopping. The following are suggestions for where the video should be stopped for discussion:

1   Show the first part of the video up to the end of the section headed *Experience*.

Discussion points:

○   People have to talk their way into getting jobs, housing or appropriate health advice. Job interviews are the most stressful kind of talking because the interviewers are judging candidates all the time.

○   The interview process is a cautious and conservative process because interviewers tend to select candidates who are like themselves.

○   Candidates' suitability is judged on their 'personality', how they 'come across'.

○   If candidates don't have the right experience, then their 'personality' and how they 'come across' will be even more important.

These points are dealt with in detail in chapters:
    3 First impressions
    4 Experience talks
    8 Coming across

2   Show the next part of the video from the heading *Questions* to the end of the section headed *Contact*.

Discussion points:

○   Long questions which elicit short answers do not help either side.

The Interview Game

o Hypothetical questions should be avoided.

o The purpose of questions is often not made clear and remains hidden.

o Having something in common means the candidate is more likely to be judged favourably.

o Sharing a joke helps to make the interviewers feel comfortable.

See chapters:

3 Show the last section of the video from *Answers* to the end. In this section, the hidden conventions of the interview game become explicit.

o One of the most important 'rules' is: sell yourself but don't be boastful.

o Candidates who do not have the right experience and need to perform especially well in *The Interview Game* are often candidates who are least likely to know the 'rules'.

o The candidate is expected to be enthusiastic rather than honest in a conventional answer.

o Doubts about candidates can lead interviewers to stop questioning and start warning candidates off the job.

The conclusion of the film is that candidates are often refused a job because they do not talk well in interviews, even if they would be good at the job.

See chapters:

9.3 *The Interview Game*: **Programme 2**

This programme is based on three sets of interviewing training sessions run for managers from Ford Motor Company and Marks and Spencer, and for personnel officers taking part in a course at South West London College. The interviews are simulations. The managers being trained on the courses are asked to interview 'candidates'. These 'candidates' are either students, or unemployed people or trainee managers already employed by the organisation. They were all aware that these were not interviews for real jobs. Each simulated interview was assessed by the trainers and the course participants.

There were two reasons why the BBC decided to film interviewing training. Firstly, it is extremely difficult to get permission to film real job interviews. The willingness to be filmed, shown by London Transport, and the candidates for the London Transport jobs, is exceptional. Secondly, the fact that training in selection interviewing is being carried out at all is a pointer to other organisations to do the same.

Programme outline
This programme has three parts. The first part shows two interviews which were part of a training course at Ford Motor Company. The second part shows three 'candidates' being interviewed by Marks and Spencer managers on a selection interviewing course. The final, and shortest, is an interview conducted by Personnel Officers at South West London College as part of their training course.

Suggestions for use
As with Programme 1 trainers are advised to stop the video after each section.

The Interview Game

1   Section one: show the two Ford interviews

Discussion points:

○   Preferred answers are those in which candidates give a mix of fact and personal opinion.

○   There should be a contract between interviewers and candidates. Interviewers should give and candidates should take every opportunity to talk freely.

○   Candidates should 'sell' themselves but not be boastful.

○   Interviewers should explicitly relate their questions to the job.

See chapters:
   2 The rules of the game
   4 Experience talks

2   Section two: show the three Marks and Spencer interviews

Discussion points:

○   Negative questioning prevents candidates from 'coming across' well. And negative information is regarded as more significant than positive information.

○   Often a whole line of questioning is obscure to candidates. (In the first Marks and Spencer interview, when the interviewer asks the candidate about where she lives, he is trying to find out how mobile she would be – whether she would be willing to move around the country.)

○   Interviewers help themselves and the candidates when they follow up open questions with more detailed questions about the candidate's past experience.

○ Candidates for white collar jobs are expected to be able to give analytical and balanced answers.

○ Active listening and feedback helps the interview to be more like a conversation and less like an interrogation.

See chapters:
   5 The hidden message
   6 Getting on together
   7 The power of questions

3   Section three: show the Personnel Officers' interview

Discussion points:

○ Interviewers have all the power in the Interview Game. Candidates often are not given even basic props such as a copy of the job description.

○ Often candidates do not know the purpose of the questions or have difficulty answering hypothetical questions.

○ Interviewers often blame candidates for their own poor performance.

See chapters:
   2 The rules of the game
   5 The hidden message
   8 Coming across

9.4   *The Interview Game* in different types of training
The Interview Game is a suitable training aid for the following types of training:

1 Selection and recruitment training for managers in the private and public sector.

2 Anti-racist training aimed at combatting institutionalised discrimination.

3 Training for job-seekers.

Whatever the type of training, there are several points which trainers need to bear in mind.

Preparation
These programmes should not be shown on their own without adequate preparation. They should be part of an extended workshop or seminar along the lines suggested below.

Any training on cross-cultural communication and issues of discrimination should be planned and delivered by black and white trainers working together.

The programmes as training aids
These programmes can raise awareness and give suggestions but they do not provide a complete answer to how interviews, particularly equal opportunities interviews, should be run. Every interview is, in some ways, unique because of the particular dynamic set up by the questions asked and answers given, so each interviewer has to find individual solutions to the problem of how to make the interview fair and effective. Nor should participants feel that because they have watched the video and discussed it, that they have 'done equal opportunities interviewing'. The issues raised in these programmes touch on some of our deepest personal, social and political beliefs. Participants are not going to change the basis on which they make judgements about people only as a result of a short training course. Trainers should consider their training successful if participants make comments at the end like this: 'I now see how much is hidden in a job interview' or 'I'll look at interviews more now from the candidate's point of view', and if participants are willing to try out different ways of conducting interviews as a result of the course.

Selection and recruitment training

This training may either be a general or introductory course on recruitment and selection or it may be a course on equal opportunities interviewing. In both cases the courses are likely to cover:

Job description
Person specification
Advertising
Shortlisting
Preparation and informal meetings with candidates
Selection interviewing

The last part of the course should include video replays of simulated interviews with realistic 'candidates' and an opportunity for proper feedback and discussion. Programme 2 is particularly suitable for this training.

In equal opportunities interview training, the course should also include information on the relevant legislation and a full discussion of the relationship between interview practice and indirect racial discrimination. This type of training is normally run over three days with a one-day follow-up several weeks later. Programme 1 is particularly suitable for this training.

Anti-racist training to combat institutionalised discrimination.

The Interview Game is also suitable for training which covers the wider field of institutionalised discrimination and which examines the systems, behaviour and attitudes which underpin it.

This type of training usually includes:

○ Exercises, films and discussion aimed at examining how policies and procedures can systematically discriminate against minority ethnic groups.

The Interview Game

○ Exercises, films and discussion to help participants examine their own culture and explore their attitudes towards different ethnic groups.

○ Role plays and simulations of activities such as interviews where decisions are made.

○ Information and exercises on inter-ethnic communication to raise awareness of different styles of communicating and to help participants experience what it is like to operate in a second language.

This type of training is usually between two and four days long.

Training for job-seekers
The Interview Game can help those on training courses who are seeking work or re-training in a new skills area. The programmes can be used as part of a module on job-seeking or interview training, and should be followed up by considerable practice and role-play Selection interviews: *A Resource Pack for Trainers and Teachers* ILT (forthcoming) is also a useful set of materials for this group. It may be helpful to start with Programme 2 to establish clearly the 'rules' of the Game and then use Programme 1 to help trainees work on specific aspects of the interview, such as dealing with hypothetical questions.

Bibliography

ARGYLE, M. 1974 *The Social Psychology of Work*. Penguin Books.

ARVEY, R. and CAMPION, J. 1982 The employment interview: a summary and review of recent research. *Personnel Psychology* **35**, 281–322.

BROWN, C. 1984 *Black and White Britain: The Third P.S.I. Survey*. Heinemann Educational Books.

BROWN, P. and LEVINSON, S. 1978 Universals in language usage: politeness phenomena *in* Goody, E. (ed) *Questions and Politeness: Strategies in Social Interaction*. Cambridge University Press.

BROWN, G. and YULE, G. 1983 *Discourse Analysis*. Cambridge University Press.

COMMISSION FOR RACIAL EQUALITY
  Guidance: 1983 *Code of Practice for the Elimination of Racial Discrimination and the Promotion of Equality of Opportunity in Employment*.
  1984 *Monitoring an Equal Opportunity Policy*.
  1984 *Equal Opportunity Employment: A Guide for Employers*.
  1985 *Positive Action and Equal Opportunity in Employment*.
  Formal information report: 1984 *Polymer Engineering Division of Dunlop Ltd, Leicester: Report of Formal Investigation*.

ERICKSON, F. and SHULTZ, J. 1982 *The Counsellor as Gatekeeper: Social Interaction in Interviews* Academic Press.

FRASER, J. MUNRO 1978 *Employment Interviewing*. Macdonald and Evans.

GREENWOOD, S. 1984 *The Effects of Contextual Cues on Cross Cultural Selection Interview Outcomes*. Unpublished M.Ed. Thesis, University of Manchester, Faculty of Education.

GRICE, P. 1975 Logic and conversation. *In* Cole, P. and Morgan, J. (eds) *Syntax and Semantics* Vol. 3 *Speech Acts*. Academic Press.

GUMPERZ, J. 1982a *Discourse Strategies*. Cambridge University Press.

GUMPERZ, J. (ed) 1982b *Language and Social Identity*. Cambridge University Press.

GUMPERZ, J., JUPP, T. and ROBERTS, C. 1979 *Crosstalk* and *Crosstalk: The Wider Perspective*. 1981 National Centre for Industrial Language Training (NCILT).

HEATH, S. BRICE, 1983 *Ways with Words: Language, Life and Work in Communities and Classrooms*. Cambridge University Press.

INDUSTRIAL LANGUAGE TRAINING (ILT) (in prep.) *Selection Interviews: A Resource Pack for Trainers and Teachers*. NCILT.

JESSUP, G. and JESSUP, H. 1975 *Selection and Assessment at Work*. Methuen.

JUPP, T., et al. 1982b Language and disadvantage: the hidden process. *In* Gumperz J. (ed) 1982b *Language and Social Identity* Cambridge University Press.

KEENAN, A. 1977 Some relationships between interviewers' personal feelings about candidates and their general evaluation of them. *Journal of Occupational Psychology* **50**, 275–283.

KOCHMAN, T. 1974 Orality and literary as factors of 'black' and 'white' communicative behaviour *International Journal of Sociology of Language* 3, 95–118.

MAYFIELD, E. 1964 The selection interview. A re-evaluation of published research. *Personnel Psychology* **17**, 239–260.

MCINTOSH, N. and SMITH, D. 1974 *The Extent of Racial Discrimination*, P.E.P. Report 547.

PEARN, M. 1981 *The Fair Use of Selection Tests*. N.F.E.R.

RODGER, A. 1974 *Seven Point Plan*. N.F.E.R., n.e. by K. Rawling. N.F.E.R.–Nelson, 1985.

SACKS, H. 1971 Unpublished lecture notes. University of California.

SACKS, H., SCHEGLOFF, E. and JEFFERSON, G. 1974 A Simplest systematics for the organisation of turn-taking for conversation. *Language 50*, 695–735.

SAYERS, P. 1983b *Topic Collaboration and Interview Skills*. M.A. dissertation. University of Lancaster.

SCHMITT, N. 1976 Social and situational determinants of interview decisions. Implications for the employment interview. *Personnel Psychology* **29**, 79–101.

SCOLLON, R. and SCOLLON, S. 1983 Face in inter-ethnic communication. *In* Richards and Schmidt (eds) *Language and Communications*. Longman.

SMITH, D. 1977 *Racial Disadvantage in Britain*. Penguin.

SPRINGBETT, B. 1958 Factors affecting the final decision in the employment interview. *Canadian Journal of Psychology* **12**, 13–22.

TANNEN, D. 1979b 'What's in a frame' surface evidence for underlying expectations. *In* Freedle, R. (ed) *New Directions in Discourse Processing*. Ablex.

TIFFIN, J. and MCCORMICK, E. 1975 *Industrial Psychology*. Allen and Unwin n.e. 1981.

WAINWRIGHT, D. 1980 *Discrimination in Employment: A Guide to Equal Opportunity* Associated Business Press.

WAINWRIGHT, D. 1980 *Learning from Uncle Sam: Equal Employment Opportunities Programmes*. Runnymede Trust.

WRIGHT, O. 1969 Summary of research on the selection interviews since 1964. *Personnel Psychology*. **22**, 391–413.

YOUNG, K. and CONNELLY, N. 1982 *Policy and Practice in the Multi-racial City*. Policy Studies Institute.